Arthur W. Pinero

The Times

A Comedy in Four Acts

Arthur W. Pinero

The Times
A Comedy in Four Acts

ISBN/EAN: 9783744661652

Printed in Europe, USA, Canada, Australia, Japan

Cover: Foto ©Thomas Meinert / pixelio.de

More available books at **www.hansebooks.com**

THE TIMES

A COMEDY

In Four Acts

By ARTHUR W. PINERO

"I don't aspire to great things, but I wish to speak of great
"things with gratitude and of mean things with indignation"

LONDON: WILLIAM HEINEMANN

MDCCCXCI

INTRODUCTORY NOTE

I HAVE long hoped that the time would arrive when an English dramatist might find himself free to put into the hands of the public the text of his play simultaneously with its representation upon the stage. Interesting as might be the publication of a play subsequent to its withdrawal from the boards of a theatre, it has seemed to me that the interest would be considerably enhanced if the play could be read at the moment when it first solicited the attention of the play-goer, the consideration of the critic. Such a course, I have felt, were it adopted as a custom, might dignify at once the calling of the actor, the craft of the playwright. It would, by documentary evidence, when the play was found to possess some intrinsic value, enable the manager to defend his *judgment, while it would always apportion fairly to actor and author their just shares of credit or of blame. It would also offer conclusive testimony as to the condition of theatrical work in this country.*

It will hardly be denied that there exists in certain places the impression that an English play is a haphazard concoction of the author, the actor, and the manager; that the manuscript of a drama, could it ever be dragged, soiled and dog-eared, from the prompter's shelf, would reveal itself as a dissolute-looking, formless thing, mercilessly scarred by the managerial blue pencil and illuminated by those innumerable interpolations with which the desperate actors have helped to lift the poor material into temporary, unhealthy popularity. The publication of plays concurrently with their stage-production, in the exact shape—save for the excision of technical stage-directions—in which they have left the author's hands, can hardly fail, therefore, to be of some value to the English theatre at large. The recent readjustment of the laws of International Copyright at length enables me to offer a Book of the Play to the public after the method which I believe to be most serviceable to

THE TIMES

THE FIRST ACT

*The scene represents a richly decorated and sumptuously
furnished room in the London house of* Mr.
Egerton-Bompas, M.P. *It is prettily divided
by three arches resting on elegant pillars, and
wealth and luxury are evident in all the appoint-
ments of the room, which looks bright and cheerful
in the afternoon light of early summer.*

The door opens, and Jelf, *a manservant in livery,
introduces* Lady Ripstow, *an aristocratic-looking
woman of about fifty, and her son* Denham, Lord
Lurgashall, *a young man of twenty-seven, with
a determined manner.*

Denham.

Lady Ripstow and Lord Lurgashall.

Jelf.

I'm aware, m'lord.

Lady Ripstow.

I think Mrs. Egerton-Bompas will see me.

JELF.

I'm sure she will, m'lady, if she's at home.

LADY RIPSTOW.

She is not at home this afternoon, I know, but she may be indoors.

JELF.

I'll ask Codrington, m'lady.

LADY RIPSTOW.

Codrington ?

JELF.

My mistress's maid's woman, m'lady. [*He goes out.*

LADY RIPSTOW.

" My mistress's maid's woman ! "   The wives of drapers have their comforts, Denham.

DENHAM.

My dear mother !

LADY RIPSTOW.

Is not Mr. Bompas a draper ?

DENHAM.

Mr. Egerton-Bompas——

LADY RIPSTOW.

Egerton !

DENHAM.

Mr. Egerton-Bompas is a draper, in a large sense.

LADY RIPSTOW.

He has a dozen shops all in a row, you mean.

DENHAM.

Fourteen, as a matter of fact.

LADY RIPSTOW.

Surely that makes him fourteen times a draper.

DENHAM.

At any rate, Beryl is not a draper.

LADY RIPSTOW.

She is a draper's daughter. If she becomes your wife she will still be a draper's daughter; if children are born to you they will be a draper's daughter's children.

DENHAM.

They will be amiable and beautiful, like Beryl.

LADY RIPSTOW.

But not perfectly patrician, like yourself. To cull an illustration from the drapery business——

DENHAM.

Pray, mother!

LADY RIPSTOW.

Beryl is cotton, you are silk; each material in itself is estimable, but cotton *and* silk beget satinet. Did you see your father this morning?

DENHAM.

Yes, in bed.

LADY RIPSTOW.

Will he countenance your engagement by calling here?

DENHAM.

He will think it over.

LADY RIPSTOW.

Was he very distressed at your account of Beryl's parents?

DENHAM.

Acutely, I admit.

LADY RIPSTOW.

Of course you made him aware that Mr. Bompas sits for the northern division of St. Swithin's?

DENHAM.

Of course.

LADY RIPSTOW.

That afforded him no relief?

DENHAM.

Not perceptibly.

LADY RIPSTOW.

You emphasised—on the Conservative side of the House?

DENHAM.

Yes. But my father's theory is that a common man's profession of Conservative principles is merely a device to rub shoulders with superior people.

LADY RIPSTOW.

Theodore is penetrating.

DENHAM.

And he anticipates that every Conservative politician who has any respect for himself will soon be driven to extreme Radicalism to find decent companionship.

LADY RIPSTOW.

Your father will *never* call here, Denham!

DENHAM.

So be it, mother.

LADY RIPSTOW.

And you are determined to make Beryl an offer of marriage?

DENHAM.

Oh, quite.

BERYL, *a sweet, unaffected girl of about twenty, enters the room, attended by* JELF, *and greets* LADY RIPSTOW *and* DENHAM *with a pleasant frankness of manner.*

BERYL.

[*Addressing* LADY RIPSTOW.] Victor, the hairdresser, has been washing mamma's head. Would you like to come upstairs?

LADY RIPSTOW.

If I may.

BERYL.

[*To* DENHAM.] Excuse me.

LADY RIPSTOW.

[*Quietly to* BERYL.] Lurgashall wishes to talk to you, I know. Let the servant show me the way.

BERYL.

Jelf——

[LADY RIPSTOW *goes from the room with* JELF *in attendance, leaving* BERYL *and* DENHAM *together.*

BERYL.

I have been answering invitations for mamma—
look! What a wearisome affair is a Season, isn't it?

DENHAM.

A Season?

BERYL.

I don't mean either of the four seasons sent by
Heaven; I mean the fifth, made by Man.

DENHAM.

The one Season honoured by a capital letter.

BERYL.

And called *the* Season. Ugh!

DENHAM.

I know you care very little for gaiety.

BERYL.

The gaiety of climbing a flight of stairs to clutch
at a haggard hostess on the landing! Do sit; we
both have to tread a great many stairs to-night, I
expect.

DENHAM.

Are you going to Lady Orillian's, by any chance?

BERYL.

No, we don't know her—I mean, of course, she
doesn't know us. This is our lot. [*Reading from a
tablet.*] The Horace Bennetts', the Stratfields', Mrs.
Peter Cathew's, Music at the Verulam Club, the
Spratt-Thompsons'. Lighter than I thought. Shall
we pass you on any of those stairs?

DENHAM.

I shall be at Mrs. Cathew's about eleven.

BERYL.

A trifle early for us.

DENHAM.

Early ?

BERYL.

H'm.   We used to go very early to such places and stay right through, but, now that papa has " got on," we arrive late everywhere and murmur an apology !

DENHAM.

Ha, ha !

BERYL.

Ah, don't laugh !   If you realised as I do the sham, the falseness, of this sort of thing you wouldn't, you couldn't laugh—you'd cry.   And one's life seems to be made up of parade and pretension—and sometimes I feel it is more than I can——Ah !   Forgive my complaining to you.

DENHAM.

You forget I am as hemmed in as yourself—bound by conventionalism, fettered by fashion.

BERYL.

You could revolt.

DENHAM.

I might rush away to shoot big game in America. That would not be declaring independence of character, that would be escaping from declaring it.

BERYL.

Are you sure you have an independent character to declare ?

DENHAM.

At least I desire to behave as an individual; at present I am a phonograph rolled up in a coat. I don't aspire to great things, but I wish to speak of great things with gratitude and of mean things with indignation.

BERYL.

It is good of you even to talk like this. And, mind, if you ever break away, I'll pray for an adventurer.

DENHAM.

You may begin to-day then.

BERYL.

Why?

DENHAM.

I am just about to break away.

BERYL.

What are you going to do?

DENHAM.

Entreat to be allowed to pay my addresses to you.

BERYL.

[*In a murmur.*] Oh!

DENHAM.

Now you guess the object of my mother's visit this afternoon.

BERYL.

We—we are in different worlds.

DENHAM.

Let us come out of our little worlds and meet each other.

BERYL.

But I—I am—nothing.

DENHAM.

Ah, I have watched you, I know you—you are an individual. Consent to marry me, and you confer upon me the gift of individuality. Answer me.

BERYL.

Lord Lurgashall——!

DENHAM.

[*Holding out his hand.*] My dear Beryl.

BERYL.

[*Laying her hand in his.*] Denham!

PERCY EGERTON-BOMPAS, *a florid, good-humoured-looking man of about fifty, with an air of great prosperity, but with an uneasy, assertive manner, enters the room together with the* HON. MONTAGUE TRIMBLE, *a pleasant-looking, bland little man, of uncertain age, scrupulously trimmed and tailored.*

BOMPAS.

Clara, here's Monty. [*Demonstratively.*] Hallo, Lurgashall, delighted to see you!

[DENHAM *shakes hands with* BOMPAS, *and exchanges nods with* TRIMBLE.

DENHAM.

How are you, Trimble?

TRIMBLE.

How are you, my dear L.?

BOMPAS.

[*To* DENHAM.] I thought my wife was here; but Berry will give you a cup of tea.   We're always in to friends like you, if we *are* in.   But, lord bless·you, when we're not entertaining we live in other people's houses—they won't let us alone! [*Taking up cards of invitation from the table.*] I'll be bound these are invites.   What did I say?   Look here—*here* they come!   "Mrs. Bulmershe"—nice woman!   "La Comtesse de Faverot"—a Countess—French, but still——!   "Mrs. Claud Cox"—oh, stockbrokers! that's nothing.   Here!   "Lady Prestwick"!   What d'ye think of that?   "Lady Prestwick, At Home, Grosvenor Gate."   Do *you* go there, eh—do you go there?

DENHAM.

Lady Prestwick is my aunt.

BOMPAS.

Aunt, is she?   Ah, then we shall meet you.   [*Laying his hand on* DENHAM'S *shoulder.*]   It's nice for us all to be in the same set.   "Music, 10 o'clock."   I don't suppose we shall be there for more than a minute; too many of these things.   [*Reading the card to himself.*]   "Lady Prestwick, At Home, Grosvenor Gate"!   Lady Prestwick!

DENHAM.

[*Quietly to* BOMPAS.] My mother is upstairs.

BOMPAS.

Lady Ripstow!   With my wife?   Ought I to go up—ought I to go up?

DENHAM.

No, no, don't trouble. The question will be referred to you by-and-by.

BOMPAS.

What question?

DENHAM.

Whether you will sanction an engagement between Beryl and myself.

BOMPAS.

You—you in love with—our Berry?

DENHAM.

Yes.

BOMPAS.

You—you——! Shall I tell her—shall I tell her?

DENHAM.

Sssh, please! I've done that myself.

[BOMPAS *cannot speak from excitement, but he grasps* DENHAM'S *hand as* Mrs. EGERTON - BOMPAS, *a bright, excitable, good-looking woman of forty enters with* LADY RIPSTOW.

MRS. BOMPAS.

[*Breathlessly to* DENHAM.] Have you asked her?

DENHAM.

Yes.

MRS. BOMPAS.

Is it—all right?

DENHAM.

Beryl has been good enough not to discourage me.

MRS. BOMPAS.

My dear boy! I—I can't help it! [*She kisses him.*]

DENHAM.

[*Smiling.*] Thank you.

> [*He joins his mother,* BERYL, *and* TRIMBLE, *who are chatting together in a group.*

BOMPAS.

[*Trembling with excitement, to* MRS. BOMPAS.] Calm yourself, calm yourself! Don't let them think we're honoured!

MRS. BOMPAS.

Oh, Percy!

BOMPAS.

Quiet, Clara! Tell Trimble to spread it about.

> [*She joins the rest.*

BOMPAS.

[*To himself.*] I'll drop a line to the *Morning Post.* The *Times* doesn't put things in when I send 'em. [*Picking up a card of invitation.*] "Mrs. Claud Cox, At Home." Wish she may get us!

> [*He tears up the card and throws it into the waste-paper basket.* LADY RIPSTOW *approaches the table at which* BOMPAS *has sat down to write.*

BOMPAS.

[*Writing.*] "Mr. Percy Egerton-Bompas presents his compliments to the Editor of the *Morning Post* ——" [*seeing* LADY RIPSTOW] Eh? I beg your pardon —it's Lady Ripstow, isn't it? [*shaking hands with her heartily.*] How's Lord Ripstow? He and I will see more of each other now, I daresay.

LADY RIPSTOW.

Have you met Lord Ripstow ?

BOMPAS.

Well—no—that is, I may have met him and passed him. Clara ! We must fix a night for a little family dinner—no outsiders—just the family. Myself, Clara, Beryl, Howard—our boy, you know—Howard will run up from Oxford; that's four Egerton-Bompases. One Denham is five—two Ripstows are seven——

LADY RIPSTOW.

Ah ! I—I think we will defer any arrangement of this kind till Lord Ripstow—has called.

MRS. BOMPAS.

Of course, Percy.

LADY RIPSTOW.

And now, if you will allow me——

BOMPAS.

What was I going to say ? Oh, this is a big thing for Denham's future.

LADY RIPSTOW.

I—I trust so.

BOMPAS.

A father in the House of Commons as well as one in the Lords; both fathers of the same way of think-ing too, both hard-and-fast Unionists, both staunch Conservatives—the only political faith for an English gentleman.

MRS. BOMPAS.

Percy !

Bompas.

[*To* Lady Ripstow.] Don't you see ? As I've only one boy—and a good, clever boy he is, thank God !—I can keep an eye on your chick as well as my own.

Lady Ripstow.

Thank you—I—I have to call in Mereworth Square; I am coming back for Lurgashall.
> [*She passes* Bompas *and speaks a word to* Mrs. Bompas.

Bompas.

[*Resuming his seat and writing.*] " —— and begs to inform him that a marriage has been arranged——"
> [Lady Ripstow *leaves the room.*

Mrs. Bompas.

Take Lady Ripstow downstairs. What are you thinking about ?

Bompas.

[*Rising.*] Eh ?
> [*He runs out after* Lady Ripstow. — Trimble, *leaving* Beryl *and* Denham *together, advances effusively to* Mrs. Bompas.

Trimble.

Dear Mrs. E-B !

Mrs. Bompas.

Oh, Monty !

Trimble.

You are very proud—h'm ?

Mrs. Bompas.

Yes, I *am* proud. Now, now what will my old

schoolfellow, Emily Spratt-Thompson, have to say?
Oh, Monty, nothing on earth shall prevent my going
to church next Sunday morning!

TRIMBLE.

Let me see; I think *I*—h'm?

MRS. BOMPAS.

Yes, you brought him to my third reception last
season. Bless you!

[BERYL *and* DENHAM *go from the room
together.*

TRIMBLE.

[*Mournfully.*] H'aah!

MRS. BOMPAS.

What are you so glum about?

TRIMBLE.

Why, dear Mrs. E-B, I suppose I experience that
mixed sensation of pain and pleasure which the
nurse feels when the infant she has taught to toddle
wriggles its little fist out of her hand, and scampers
off unassisted.

MRS. BOMPAS.

You mean that now Berry is to make this tremendous marriage, we shall be able to run alone
in Society.

TRIMBLE.

I am unselfish enough to hope so, dear Mrs.
E-B.

MRS. BOMPAS.

But we're not likely to forget your little services,
Monty.

TRIMBLE.

No, no—you're too amiable for that. But I anticipate that your poor friend will not be quite so—so
indispensable in the future, h'm ?

MRS. BOMPAS.

Perhaps not, in the sense you mean.

TRIMBLE.

In point of fact, dear Mrs. E-B, the devoted nurse
forfeits her place and her perquisites, and the thrift-
less, improvident old woman—if I may so allude to
myself—dooced well can't afford it.

MRS. BOMPAS.

Nonsense ! Doesn't your brother—doesn't Lord
Morphett do something for you ?

TRIMBLE.

Dear Morphett pays the allowance I am compelled
to make my wife—that's all. But as for the neces-
saries of life, I pledge you my word, there was a
moment last September when the question of my
giving up my little box in Scotland was really mooted.
However, I was fortunate enough to get you and
E-B some pleasant introductions at Homburg, and
the dear liberal fellow——

MRS. BOMPAS.

Yes, yes—never mind that.

TRIMBLE.

But now—

MRS. BOMPAS.

Sssh ! I'll tell Percy to be always very kind to you.

TRIMBLE.

Dear soul!

MRS. BOMPAS.

I can't sit still, Monty!

[*She moves restlessly about the room.*

TRIMBLE.

I came here this afternoon to give you what I hoped would prove a piece of good news.

MRS. BOMPAS.

There's no more good news in the world!

TRIMBLE.

No, not *now*.

MRS. BOMPAS.

Well, what is it?

TRIMBLE.

The Maharaja of Shikapoor has at last fixed a night to dine here.

MRS. BOMPAS.

What! you've got him!

TRIMBLE.

After shockin' difficulties.

MRS. BOMPAS.

Oh, bless you, bless you, dear man! Now, now, Emily Spratt-Thompson, what will you have to say!

[BOMPAS *returns.*]

MRS. BOMPAS.

Percy, that nigger has consented to dine with us!

B

BOMPAS.

The Maharaja ?

MRS. BOMPAS.

Yes.

BOMPAS.

No !   Has he ?   When ?

TRIMBLE.

The 20th.

BOMPAS.

Ours is the first private house this great Indian potentate will have dined at.

TRIMBLE.

Certainly.

MRS. BOMPAS.

Hah ! triumph !

TRIMBLE.

Led by some association of ideas he has hitherto persisted in going every night to the Empire.

MRS. BOMPAS.

Percy, it must be a brilliant occasion.

BOMPAS.

By Jove, yes !   Monty !

TRIMBLE.

Command me, dear E-B.   Now, whom will you have to meet the great man—your friends ?

BOMPAS.

Friends ?

MRS. BOMPAS.

Friends ?

BOMPAS.

You see, one can always have friends.

TRIMBLE.

But you want to let your friends see you've got the Maharaja.

BOMPAS.

No, no, no—they'll read about it in the papers.

MRS. BOMPAS.

I should like the best people in London.

TRIMBLE.

The best we can get.

BOMPAS.

Clara, we will make this the dinner to which we ask the Ripstows—Lord and Lady Ripstow. We'll shew them, hey? We'll let them see, shall we?

MRS. BOMPAS.

But you told Lady Ripstow that their dinner was to be a family dinner.

BOMPAS..

[*Quietly to her.*] Yes, but I've been thinking—they might expect to meet my relations.

TRIMBLE.

I've already roughed out a few suggestions.

BOMPAS.

Good!

MRS. BOMPAS.

Monty is so useful.

TRIMBLE.

[*Consulting his memoranda.*] Now, there's old Lord Hipgrave——

MRS. BOMPAS.

Lord Hipgrave!

BOMPAS.

Lord Hipgrave! Phew!

TRIMBLE.

I can get *him*.

BOMPAS.

I shall be happy to welcome Lord Hipgrave to my house.

TRIMBLE.

He's not in demand just now, and will eat a good dinner anywhere. But he's still a great name, dear Mrs. E-B.

MRS. BOMPAS.

Tremendous!

TRIMBLE.

I feel bound to tell you that he feeds in rather a coarse way——

MRS. BOMPAS.

Disgusting!

BOMPAS.

Sssh! he's a great name!

TRIMBLE.

[*Reading from his notes.*] And he begs that—oh, here it is—he begs that a dinner may not be held to constitute acquaintanceship.

BOMPAS.

Infernal impudence!

MRS. BOMPAS.

The brutes that dine at my table!

BOMPAS.

However, he's a great name. Well!

TRIMBLE.

Sir Charles Farmiloe will come with Algy Fitzbray.

BOMPAS.

Excellent!

TRIMBLE.

Just for fun, is the way they put it.

MRS. BOMPAS.

Cads!

TRIMBLE.

They are mere boys, you know, and never open their lips. Then there's Charley Spreckly—he will whip the thing up.

BOMPAS.

By Jove, rather!

MRS. BOMPAS.

Oh! He tells all these inimitable stories; they're in everybody's mouth.

TRIMBLE.

Well, everybody's inimitable stories are in *his* mouth—same thing. He's the best *raconteur* in society.

BOMPAS.

[*To* MRS. BOMPAS.] Know we should get him some day.

TRIMBLE.

But I ought to let you know, dear E-B, that Spreckly asks five-and-twenty guineas.

MRS. BOMPAS.

What!

BOMPAS.

From every house he goes to?

TRIMBLE.

From *some* houses he goes to.   It is kept absolutely quiet, of course; if such a thing got about, he might as well go on the stage at once.

MRS. BOMPAS.

Five-and-twenty——!

TRIMBLE.

Yes, and you don't get his *new* stories for that.

BOMPAS.

Pay him thirty—this must be a perfect dinner.

MRS. BOMPAS.

Now, the women.

TRIMBLE.

That's always a little difficulty, h'm?   You wouldn't care for a cheerful but perfectly lady-like actress?

MRS. BOMPAS.

[*Reproachfully.*] My dear Monty!

TRIMBLE.

I beg pardon.

MRS. BOMPAS.

Really, I would much rather ask my own personal friends.

TRIMBLE.

Have you your Visiting List handy?

[*She gives him a book from the table.*

TRIMBLE.

I daresay there are some good people here you don't know. I'll run through it in the next room; it may give my brain a fillip.

[*He goes out. JELF enters.*

JELF.

Carriage is at the door, sir.

[*JELF withdraws.*

MRS. BOMPAS.

Going down to the House, Percy?

BOMPAS.

Yes, dear.

[*They sit cosily together, and she arranges a flower in his buttonhole.*

BOMPAS.

May I drive you anywhere?

MRS. BOMPAS.

No, thanks. I've asked Miss Cazalet to pop in.

BOMPAS.

Kate Cazalet, the novelist?

MRS. BOMPAS.

Yes. I hear she's become the proprietress of a struggling little daily newspaper — the *Morning Message.*

BOMPAS.

Never heard of it—won't live. A woman, too!

MRS. BOMPAS.

Isn't it ridiculous! Still, one may get one's gowns decently described ; so I thought a cup of tea in a friendly, informal way——

BOMPAS.

Very good-natured of you, I'm sure. Give her my best wishes.

MRS. BOMPAS.

[*Laying her hand upon his arm as he is going.*] Percy, dear, are they beginning to make you feel more at home in the House ?

BOMPAS.

Well—— !

MRS. BOMPAS.

I wonder, darling, if your manner strikes them as being a little too—a little too pushing.

BOMPAS.

I shouldn't be surprised. But, you see, it's the only manner I've got.

MRS. BOMPAS.

I know, dear, I know.

BOMPAS.

And it comes natural to me. And if I don't push, Clara, I feel, somehow, that I'm not " in it."

MRS. BOMPAS.

But you *are* " in it," Percy. We're wealthy, with

a town house and a country one, with horses, carriages, servants, and twice as much of everything as we need. You should remind yourself of this constantly.

BOMPAS.

I do, I do, every minute of the day. I believe I'm sensitive, Clara.

MRS. BOMPAS.

About what ?

BOMPAS.

Perhaps it's—the business.

MRS. BOMPAS.

The business will soon be a Company—" Bompas's Limited "—and you the Chairman.

BOMPAS.

Ah, but I've walked the shop a good deal in my time and—it's the same with a man that's been to sea—that tells its own tale. The other night I was bustling across the Members' lobby, in my own energetic way, you know, and I heard a voice near me saying, " What price, blankets ? "

MRS. BOMPAS.

Infamous !

BOMPAS.

Of course it proceeded from an Irish member, but still——

Mrs. BOMPAS.

Not Mr. McShane again ? .

BOMPAS.

Yes, that little beast, McShane. And then, ingratitude hurts me. I've been in the House a couple

of months, and what's the one question on which my
opinion has been sought, the one point I've been
consulted upon?

MRS. BOMPAS.

Yes, yes, you've told me.

BOMPAS.

The quality of the table-linen in the dining-room.
Hah! However, wait! wait!

MRS. BOMPAS.

Bless you.

BOMPAS.

Well, good-bye, old lady.

MRS. BOMPAS.

[*Putting her arms round his neck.*]   Good-bye, poor
old man.   [*Brushing a tear away.*]   After all—we're
very lucky, aren't we?

BOMPAS.

Rather—and deserve to be.

> [MRS. BOMPAS *sits at the table, humming a*
> *song happily.*

BOMPAS.

Oh, I want my copy of the Labour Bill—it's in the
library.

> JELF *enters quietly, and approaches* BOMPAS.   *They*
> *speak together unheard by* MRS. BOMPAS.

JELF.

[*In a whisper.*] Sir.

BOMPAS.

What is it?

JELF.

[*Looking towards* MRS. BOMPAS.] Hush, please, sir!
Mr. Howard's come home.

BOMPAS.

Mr. Howard!

JELF.

I'm afraid everything's not quite right, sir—he
cried when he saw me.

BOMPAS.

Where is he?

JELF.

In the library, sir—with some ladies.

BOMPAS.

With some—out of the way!

> [BOMPAS *goes out hurriedly, followed by*
> JELF. BERYL AND DENHAM *come into
> the room.*

MRS. BOMPAS.

Well, darlings?

BERYL.

Lord Lurgashall asked me to show him Richmond's
portrait of myself, mamma.

MRS. BOMPAS.

Bless her! And did you notice Holl's picture of
Mr. Egerton-Bompas, in the dining-room?

DENHAM.

Oh, yes.

Mrs. Bompas.

Doesn't it speak! We intend bequeathing it to the Carlton Club.

[*The door opens.*

Jelf.

[*Announcing*] Miss Cazalet—Miss Tuck.

[Jelf *shows in* Miss Cazalet, *a vivacious, handsome, well-preserved and richly attired woman of about seven-and-thirty, and* Lucy, *a pale, sadlooking girl, wearing spectacles, and almost shabbily dressed.*

Mrs. Bompas.

[*Kissing* Miss Cazalet.] So good of you to come!

Miss Cazalet.

What a charming house you have! [*To* Beryl.] How are you, dear?

Mrs. Bompas.

Do you know Lord Lurgashall?

Miss Cazalet.

By his likeness to his papa, not otherwise. [Denham *bows formally.*] Lucy, dear. [*To* Mrs. Bompas.] I so want to introduce my little niece, Lucy Tuck.

Mrs. Bompas.

[*To* Lucy.] How do you do?

MISS CAZALET.

Poor Lucy has broken down wofully at Newnham. Her feminine intellect has drawn the line at Latin Prose, and left her rubbing menthol into her brows from morning till night.

MRS. BOMPAS.

Dear child!

BERYL.

[*Sympathetically.*] Oh, mamma!

MISS CAZALET.

[*To* BERYL.] You girls are nearly of the same age —do tell her there is something in the world besides a First Class in the Classical Tripos.

BERYL.

[*To* LUCY.] And have you a bad head this afternoon?

LUCY.

Oh, yes.

BERYL.

When did it come on?

LUCY.

The year before last.

BERYL.

The year before last?

LUCY.

It isn't of so much consequence now I've left Newnham, only they say it makes me appear unsociable.

Miss Cazalet.

[*To* Mrs. Bompas, *who has been chatting with her apart.*] A thousand congratulations! May I announce it in my paper?

Mrs. Bompas.

Do.

Miss Cazalet.

Any date fixed?

Mrs. Bompas.

[*In a whisper.*] Not yet.

Miss Cazalet.

By-the-way, I hope you all know that anybody who buys a copy of the *Morning Message* on and after Monday is bestowing a penny upon a hardworking, deserving woman. The *Morning Message*—ever heard of it?

Denham.

I must confess I——

Miss Cazalet.

Ah, I thought not.

Jelf *enters, carrying a silver tray with tea-things.* Beryl *pours out tea.*

Miss Cazalet.

Poor little journal—it's only six months old and very weak, like a rickety baby! I'm going to nurse it into vitality. [*To* Denham.] Isn't it bold, eh?

Denham.

Extremely.

MISS CAZALET.

You mean brazen ! [*Catching* BERYL's *eye.*] Two
lumps, please, dear, and cream.

MRS. BOMPAS.

You must be careful not to lose your money.

MISS CAZALET.

Oh, that's all right. A dear good friend in the
City, who believes in me, has bought the paper for
that [*snapping her fingers*], and has given it to me as
a—as a birthday present.

> [DENHAM *hands* MISS CAZALET *a cup of
> tea : she declines cake.*

MISS CAZALET.

No, thanks; I'm too full of the *Morning Message*
to eat— excuse my coarseness.

DENHAM.

H'm !

MISS CAZALET.

My City friend furnishes the Money Article,
naturally.

DENHAM.

[*To himself.*] I'll be bound he does.

MISS CAZALET.

I do Society, the Opera and the Play, and perhaps
Ascot and Cowes.

MRS. BOMPAS.

Don't overtax yourself, dear.

MISS CAZALET.

Oh, of course I have a man Editor and all sorts of nice things of that kind about me—to save me the fag, you know.

MRS. BOMPAS.

[*Taking tea.*] Thanks. And you think a woman really possesses the authority—— ?

MISS CAZALET.

Authority! Why the staff already kiss the ground I walk on. At 18 Boswell Court, second floor—office of the *M. M.*—I'm a queen, my dears, inky but absolute. It's glorious!

MRS. BOMPAS.

And so, on Monday——

MISS CAZALET.

And every morning, you'll each buy the *Message*, please—my *Message!* [*To each and all.*] Will you? Will you? Will you?

MRS. BOMPAS, DENHAM, BERYL.

Certainly.

MISS CAZALET.

Thanks, awfully. Three-pence! [*Quietly to* MRS. BOMPAS.] Oh, may I speak to you, dear?

MRS. BOMPAS.

Quietly?

MISS CAZALET.

[*To* LUCY.] Lucy, I want you to tell dear Mrs. Egerton-Bompas—come here.

[MISS CAZALET *and* LUCY *talk confidentially with* MRS. BOMPAS.

BERYL.

[*To* DENHAM, *handing his tea.*]   What is your impression of Miss Cazalet?

DENHAM.

[*Sipping his tea.*] Sweet.

BERYL.

Really?

DENHAM.

The tea.

BERYL.

Who is she?   I don't think we know her very well.

DENHAM.

She is one of Sir George Cazalet's many beautiful daughters.

BERYI.

Quite a lady, then?

DENHAM.

He was quite a gentleman.   .

BERYL.

What has been her career?

DENHAM.

After poor old Sir George's death she wrote realistic novels, until——

BERYL.

Until——?

DENHAM.

Until realism was exhausted, Mudie alienated, and Smith shocked.

BERYL.

Why this journalistic craze?

DENHAM.

Oh, morphia, brandy, or ink — all uneradicable habits in a woman.

BERYL.

I see you don't like her.

DENHAM.

Well—I'd rather you did not. Good gracious! It has just struck me—suppose my mother finds her here! It can't be helped.

BERYL.

What do you mean?

DENHAM.

It's an absurd old story, Beryl—may I confide it to you? This lady was once included in a country-house party with my mother and father. It pleased my dear mother, who is a woman, to be ridiculously jealous.

BERYL.

Of Miss Cazalet?

DENHAM.

The affair was perfectly foundationless, but my father, as an assertion of his independence, thought proper when he returned to town—to call.

BERYL.

On Miss Cazalet?

DENHAM.

Yes. Ever since then my mother has hated——

BERYL.

Not your father!

DENHAM.

No—Miss Cazalet.

BERYL.

Hark! Is that Lady Ripstow's carriage?

[BERYL and DENHAM *look out of window.*

MRS. BOMPAS.

[*To* MISS CAZALET.] I declare, it's quite sweet of you.

MISS CAZALET.

No, no—I regard my poor niece as a very precious responsibility. But she would be so much happier for some employment—not the newspaper, the mere mention of that makes her head fall in two—something placid, something mouselike.

MRS. BOMPAS.

[*Making notes.*] I'll consult Percy. You suggest——?

MISS CAZALET.

She would be a soothing companion for an old lady.

MRS. BOMPAS.

There are so many old ladies, too.

MISS CAZALET.

Yes, if they'd only admit it. Or as tutor to some backward or delicate girl.

MRS. BOMPAS.

There!

MISS CAZALET.

You dear woman! [*producing a note-book.*] What gown do you wear at the opera on Saturday night?

MRS. BOMPAS.

One of Mrs. Weatherhill's. The skirt is yellow
silk brocaded with tiny pompadour bouquets of
flowers. Round the hem, three festooned flounces of
pale yellow chiffon——

> [JELF *shows in* LADY RIPSTOW *and withdraws.*

LADY RIPSTOW.

Has Lurgashall gone?

MRS. BOMPAS.

No.

> [MISS CAZALET *looks up from her note-book;
> she and* LADY RIPSTOW *recognise each
> other.*

MRS. BOMPAS.

[*To* LADY RIPSTOW.] Let me introduce my friend,
Miss Cazalet.

MISS CAZALET.

[*Offering her hand.*] I think we've met before,
haven't we?

> [LADY RIPSTOW *regards her with a cold
> stare, then turns to* DENHAM.

LADY RIPSTOW.

Denham——

MISS CAZALET.

[*To* LUCY.] She cut me! That woman cut me!
Oh, if ever I have the chance——!

> [BOMPAS *enters the room, his face pale, his
> hair disordered, his manner much dis-
> composed.*

Mrs. Bompas.

Percy!

Bompas.

[*Whispering to her.*] Get rid of 'em, get rid of 'em!

Lady Ripstow.

[*To* Mrs. Bompas.] Good-bye. [*To* Bompas.] Good-bye!

Bompas.

Good-bye, Lady Ripstow. Remember me to Lord Ripstow, I beg. What was I going to say?

[Lady Ripstow *goes out with* Beryl.

Denham.

[*Shaking hands with* Mr. *and* Mrs. Bompas.] We shall meet to-night, I hope.

Bompas.

Somewhere or other—somewhere or other.

[Denham *goes out.*

Miss Cazalet.

[*Shaking hands with* Mrs. Bompas.] Good-bye, dear.

Mrs. Bompas.

Must you go? So sorry.

[Mrs. Bompas *rings the bell.*

Bompas.

[*Shaking hands with* Miss Cazalet.] Good luck to your paper—meets a want—I was saying so this afternoon.

Miss Cazalet.

How well you're looking ! Good-bye !

[Jelf *appears, and shows* Miss Cazalet *and* Lucy *out.*

Mrs. Bompas.

What's the matter ?

Bompas.

[*Wildly.*] The matter !

Mrs. Bompas.

[*Shaking his arm.*] Percy !

Trimble *enters, with the visiting-list and some sheets of paper, but remains in the background.*

Mrs. Bompas.

Percy ! Speak to me !

Bompas.

Howard !

Mrs. Bompas.

My boy ! There's something wrong ! You've got a letter from him ! Percy, he's not ill ! He's not—— !

Bompas.

Worse—married !

Mrs. Bompas.

Married ! My child—married !

Bompas.

Hah !

Mrs. Bompas.

Married—whom !

BOMPAS.

Say *what!* A nobody—a nothing—an ignorant, ill-bred hussy!

MRS. BOMPAS.

No, no!

BOMPAS.

A low trollop you daren't show to your friends—a slut that's not good enough for our kitchen!

[MRS. BOMPAS *throws herself upon the settee in hysterics, as* BERYL *enters.*

MRS. BOMPAS.

Oh dear, oh dear, oh dear! Ha, ha, ha, ha! Oh dear, oh dear, oh dear!

BERYL.

Mamma!

TRIMBLE.

My dear Mrs. E-B!

MRS. BOMPAS.

My boy—my child—my poor boy!

BOMPAS.

Be quiet!

BERYL.

What has happened?

MRS. BOMPAS.

Your brother has married somebody.

BERYL.

Married!

MRS. BOMPAS.

Ha, ha, ha!

BOMPAS.

Monty, we can trust you; Beryl, hold your tongue!

BERYL.

[*To* TRIMBLE.] A little water!

> [TRIMBLE *runs out,* BERYL *holds a vinai-*
> *grette to* MRS. BOMPAS'S *nose.*

BOMPAS.

Disgraced! disgraced! Just as I was getting on!

BERYL.

Be silent, papa!

BOMPAS.

Cards flowing in—flowing in—from the best people!
The Maharaja about to dine here! And Lurgashall
—just as we are engaged to Lurgashall! It will fall
through!

BERYL.

Oh, don't! Look at mamma!

BOMPAS.

Look at mamma! Look at *me!*

TRIMBLE *re-enters hurriedly with a glass of water—*
BOMPAS *stretches out his hand for it.*

BOMPAS.

Ah!

TRIMBLE.

No, no, it's for your wife.

BOMPAS.

Oh ! It will be broken off—our engagement—to Lurgashall—broken off !

[MRS. BOMPAS *recovers, and sits up faintly.*

MRS. BOMPAS.

[*To* BOMPAS.] Tell me.

BOMPAS.

It appears that Howard hasn't been near Oxford for more than a couple of months.

MRS. BOMPAS.

But we've received letters from him written on his club paper.

BOMPAS.

Asking for supplies—hah, he managed that.

BERYL.

Where has he been, papa ?

BOMPAS.

At that little out-of-the-way hole in Wales——

BERYL.

Llannyllyth ?

BOMPAS.

Llannyllyth, where he and young Parker and Giltspur went to read. To read !

MRS. BOMPAS.

I told you I didn't believe in reading-parties. He'd much better have come home to learn his lessons —I'd have found time to hold the book for him.

BOMPAS.

Well, the other fellows, Parker and Giltspur, returned to college——

MRS. BOMPAS.

Without Howard ?

BOMPAS.

Yes, he made some excuse to remain behind.
Faugh !

MRS. BOMPAS.

Why ?

BOMPAS.

Why !   Why !

BERYL.

Papa, don't !

TRIMBLE.

My dear, E-B !

BOMPAS.

Why !   So that he might marry—so that he might
marry—his landlady's daughter.

MRS. BOMPAS.

His landlady's——!

BOMPAS.

The daughter of a common creature named Dooley
or Hooley—an Irish widow.

MRS. BOMPAS.

Irish !

BOMPAS.

A pauper who seems to have got stuck in the mud at Llannyllyth, on her way from Ireland, for want of funds. Funds! The dear lady's got another to keep now!

MRS. BOMPAS.

Oh, no, no!

BOMPAS.

[*Staring before him wildly.*] There will be one lodging-house at Llannyllyth where a young man is engaged to clean boots and windows!

BERYL.

Papa!

TRIMBLE.

Really, E-B!

BOMPAS.

Apartments for families—pleasant view of the glorious vale of Llannyllyth! Door opened by my boy's wife's mother, in curl-papers! Chambermaid, my daughter-in-law! Only lodging-house in the Principality with a butler—my son and heir!

BERYL.

Papa, you are exaggerating! If there is any truth at all in this horrid report—

BOMPAS.

Truth!

BERYL.

I am certain the reality is far less terrible than the story you tell us. Let us read it for ourselves— show us the letter.

BOMPAS.

The letter !

BERYL.

Isn't there a letter ?   How do you know all this ?

BOMPAS.

Oh, yes, of course—I haven't mentioned—

HOWARD EGERTON-BOMPAS, *a commonplace, heavy young man, of about one-and-twenty, looking very wretched and upset, enters quietly.*

HOWARD.

Ma !

MRS. BOMPAS.

Oh !

BERYL.

Howard !

HOWARD.

I want to know what's going to be done.

MRS. BOMPAS.

[*Kissing him.*] My boy !

HOWARD.

All right, ma dear.   I s'pose you've heard all about it.

BERYL.

Papa has told us.

HOWARD.

Hullo, Monty !

TRIMBLE.

Er—um—ah—good afternoon.

HOWARD.

Here's a mess, Monty.

TRIMBLE.

You are right, dear young friend.

MRS. BOMPAS.

Oh, Howard, whatever made you do a thing like this?

HOWARD.

I dun' know.

BERYL.

You must know, Howard.

HOWARD.

Well, I s'pose a sort of lonely feeling came over me —I dun' know. And then I got fogged over my Constitutional Law—I dun' know. And then my head seemed to swell. And then Honoria—

MRS. BOMPAS.

Honoria?

HOWARD.

My wife.

MRS. BOMPAS.

Ah!

HOWARD.

Honoria used to lay the cloth.

MRS. BOMPAS.

Yes?

HOWARD.

Well, Honoria used to lay the cloth.

MRS. BOMPAS.

You've said that, darling.

HOWARD.

Well, Honoria used to lay the cloth — and so I married her at the Registry Office.

MRS. BOMPAS.

Not even in church ?

HOWARD.

I'm telling you—at the little Registry Office at Abergaron. It can't get about; my chums never guessed I was in love, and my two witnesses were a deaf gardener and a chalk labourer; and I can hook it to Australia, or the Cape, and our fine friends won't be a bit the wiser. And if people ask what's become of me, you can say—well, I dun' know.

MRS. BOMPAS.

[*Putting her arms around his neck.*] Australia !

HOWARD.

Oh, let a fellow breathe !

MRS. BOMPAS.

You stifle him, Beryl. Tell me, what is she like?

HOWARD.

Jolly pretty, *I* think.

BERYL.

Is she fairly educated, Howard?

HOWARD.

What does that matter ?

BERYL.

Oh, Howard !

HOWARD.

No, she's *not* fairly educated. I've tried to teach her how to spell a little, and I've found out I don't know how to spell, myself. So *I'm* not fairly educated; and I suppose you'd call me a representative young English gentleman.

MRS. BOMPAS.

And—and—the mother?

HOWARD.

Mrs. Hooley?

MRS. BOMPAS.

Is she—nice?

HOWARD.

I dun' know.

BERYL.

You must know, Howard.

HOWARD.

Look here, one would think I was being ragged by the Warden! I won't stand it! Recollect, I—I— I'm a married man!

BOMPAS.

Now then, now then, how dare you!

HOWARD.

You see I'm upset. If you want to quiz my new people, and—and—disparage them, they're sitting in the library——

MRS. BOMPAS.

Here!

BERYL.

Mamma!

MRS. BOMPAS.

Percy, why haven't I been told this? I demand to see my son's wife! Take me downstairs, instantly!

BOMPAS.

No, no—not another scene there, with a couple of servants in the hall. I'll—no—Monty, you're a stranger, they won't howl so much with you. Get 'em out of the library and sneak 'em up here.

[TRIMBLE *goes out.*

MRS. BOMPAS.

Why didn't you bring your wife alone? Why the mother? Surely the mother would have kept for a week or two.

HOWARD.

I didn't want to bring Mrs. Hooley. Do you think I'm a fool?

BERYL.

For shame, Howard!

HOWARD.

Why, I hadn't the cash to bring anybody. I was stoney-broke; you can't marry without extra expenses. It's Mrs. Hooley who's brought *me!*— third-class too, like a cad!

BOMPAS.

I hear them! Ahhh! quiet! quiet!

MRS. BOMPAS.

Is my hair all right, Beryl?

BERYL.

Yes, mamma.   [TRIMBLE *returns.*

TRIMBLE.

Come in, pray come in!

[HONORIA, *an ordinarily pretty Irish girl of about eighteen, rather showily dressed, and* MRS. HOOLEY, *her mother, a " genteel " person of eight-and-thirty, not very tidy in appearance, enter timidly amid gloomy silence. They have both been weeping.*

TRIMBLE.

I think Mr.—and Mrs.—Egerton-Bompas would like you to sit down.

BOMPAS.

[*To* HONORIA *and* MRS. HOOLEY.] Be seated.

[HONORIA *and* MRS. HOOLEY *sit, and continue sobbing at intervals.*

MRS. BOMPAS.

Mrs. —— ?

MRS. HOOLEY.

[*Speaking with a slight brogue.*] Hooley — Kathleen Hooley, widow of Captain Patrick Fagan Hooley.

BOMPAS.

Captain?

MRS. HOOLEY.

Captain of the coastguard at Kilbrain, north of Ireland. He fell into the water fifteen years ago in time to be spared the trouble that's come upon us.

MRS. BOMPAS.

Trouble that's *come* upon us! You've *brought* it on us!

MRS. HOOLEY.

Indeed I've not, ma'am!

BOMPAS.

Pooh!

MRS. HOOLEY.

No, sir, I've not; and though I'm a widow in trifling circumstances, and haven't a living relation but my one child, I wouldn't have sought to better myself by bringing distress upon gentlefolk—not to wear a coronet upon my brow!

HONORIA.

That's true, ma'am. It's been all the sly doing of me and the young gentleman. Why did I consent to it?

MRS. HOOLEY.

I was away from Llannyllyth for a couple of days, ma'am, leaving the cottage in Honoria's keeping while I took the cattle-boat to Kilbrain to inquire after a little furniture I'd stored there years ago.

BOMPAS.

Yah! bah, bah!

MRS. HOOLEY.

And when I got home last night, slightly prematurely, I looked up at my cottage and saw but one light burning, and that in my own modest sitting-room. And I said to myself, "the young gentleman's fatigued with his reading, and he's gone to bed with an aching head, that's evident."

MRS. BOMPAS.

Well, well, well!

Mrs. Hooley.

So I let myself in with my key and walked quietly into my modest sitting-room, and there I saw Honoria, on one side of the table, darning the young gentleman's socks, and the young gentleman himself ỏn the other side with a pipe in his mouth and his feet resting on the mantelpiece among my little ornaments and lustres.

Bompas.

Last night! You haven't lost much time in paying us a visit.

Mrs. Hooley.

No, sir, because I thought the sooner the entire family had a meeting the better.

Bompas.

The entire——!

Mrs. Hooley.

So that we might all look one another in the face, sir, as we are now doing, and put a simple question to each other.

Mrs. Bompas.

A question?

Mrs. Hooley.

The question, ma'm—what is to be done?

Bompas.

I'll answer that——!

Beryl.

Papa dear. Let me make the first suggestion. [*Sitting beside* Honoria.] Oh, do please let me!

BOMPAS.

Clara!

MRS. BOMPAS.

Beryl!

BERYL.

It is, that we answer the question, " What is to be done ? " [*taking* HONORIA'S *hand*] by deciding to make the best of it.

HONORIA.

Oh !

MRS. HOOLEY.

My dear young lady !

BOMPAS.

How dare you, how dare you, how dare you !

MRS. BOMPAS.

Percy ! Percy !

[BERYL *quickly takes* HONORIA *and* MRS. HOOLEY *apart; they are joined by* HOWARD, *and talk together in whispers.*

BOMPAS.

How dare she !   A nice couple of children I've got. One marries a trollop, the other—the other makes the best of it !

MRS. BOMPAS.

I don't know what's come over her.   [*Joining the others.*]   Beryl !

BOMPAS.

The best of it !   The best of it !   Hah, the best of it !   [*Glaring at* TRIMBLE, *who is quietly eating lumps of sugar.*]   Complacent ass !   [*To* TRIMBLE.]   Well ?

TRIMBLE.

My sweet tooth.

BOMPAS.

I'm glad my misfortunes don't affect you.

TRIMBLE.

On the contrary, dear E-B, I was just thinking——

BOMPAS.

Thinking.   Not of a way out of it ?

TRIMBLE.

No, no—of a way *round* it.

BOMPAS.

Eh ?

TRIMBLE.

Being a non-smoker, munching always helps me to
ponder, and I was recalling a case in point.

BOMPAS.

A case in point ?   Case in——?   Similar ?

TRIMBLE.

Well, it was the instance of a dear friend of mine
—a member of the Upper House, by-the-by—a dear
friend of mine, whose boy, having fallen in love with
a common little provincial shop-girl, did the wrong
thing by her and surreptitiously married her.

BOMPAS.

That's similar.   A peer too—it happens to the
best of us !   Well ?

TRIMBLE.

Well, *that* girl was unencumbered by relatives——

BOMPAS.

Like—— ?

TRIMBLE.

Like these good people.　It was hearing the widow say she's minus relations that put this old affair into my head.　[*Taking another piece of sugar.*]　Excuse me.

BOMPAS.

But what was done ?　What was done ?　What was done ?

TRIMBLE.

Why, my dear old friend, Lord—but I must be careful—my dear old friend hit upon a somewhat daring idea.　He never revealed the circumstance of his son's clandestine marriage.

BOMPAS.

What good did that——?

TRIMBLE.

Wait.　Keeping this marriage a secret, he created for the poor girl, entirely out of his imagination, a decent if not distinguished parentage and a thoroughly creditable past, into which, owing to its fictitiousness, it was naturally impossible for his friends to pry.

BOMPAS.

He pretended the girl—was a—lady, you mean ?

TRIMBLE.

Certainly—and he made her one.　He took her to

his heart—dear fellow!—had her manners and her orthography duly polished, and eventually he presented to the world as the *fiancée* of his son a young person fitted in all outward essentials to adorn Society.

BOMPAS.

By Jove!

TRIMBLE.

The wedding took place at St. Peter's, Seaton Square. Everybody was radiant and happy, especially the boy's father.

BOMPAS.

The father!

TRIMBLE.

Yes — pardonably proud of having saved Society from a scandal and his son from a *mésalliance*.

BOMPAS.

But it was a fraud, a cheat, a humbug!

TRIMBLE.

Well, well — but everybody was benefited. Of course, I really ought not to have mentioned it, dear E-B, only the likeness between the two cases——

BOMPAS.

But *you* wouldn't—if *you* had a boy who made a fool of himself—you wouldn't—you wouldn't—would you?

TRIMBLE.

Dear friend, I frankly own that in such a predicament I should do all a father could do to—to--to preserve his son's self-respect.

BOMPAS.

Oh !

TRIMBLE.

It was in that parental spirit that I assisted Lord ——, my other dear old friend.

BOMPAS.

You—you helped him ?

TRIMBLE.

Yes.   [*Taking another lump of sugar.*]

BOMPAS.

[*To himself.*] No, no—*you'd* do it, but *I* wouldn't. After all, fair trade hasn't done so badly for me, and, if it wasn't for Clara, I sometimes think I'd—I'd——

[Mrs. HOOLEY's *voice rises discordantly above the others for a moment.*

BOMPAS.

Ugh ! Monty ! Tell me your plan again ! Tell me again !

END OF THE FIRST ACT.

THE SECOND ACT

The scene is still the reception-room at the EGERTON
BOMPAS'S; *it is a summer morning, a month later
than the events of the preceding Act.*

MRS. BOMPAS *sits alone, meditating upon a letter she
holds in her hand. She does not notice* JELF, *who
stands by the door awaiting her orders.*

JELF.

The bell rang, ma'am.

MRS. BOMPAS.

Eh? Oh, yes. Tell them upstairs that Miss
Mountrafford's new governess arrives to-day at—
what time? Where is Miss Cazalet's note? Oh!
[*reading to herself*] "Dearest Mrs. Egerton-Bompas,
how delightful of you to offer to take my little niece
into your household as Miss Mountrafford's help and
companion. As for Lucy, she is dying to devote
herself to your son's charming *fiancée*. I'll bring her
to you myself to-morrow morning at eleven——" [*to*
JELF] Miss Tuck will be here at eleven.

JELF.

Yes, ma'am.

[JELF *leaves the room as* BERYL *comes in,
dressed for going out.*

BERYL.

[*Coldly.*] Good morning, mamma.

MRS. BOMPAS.

Are you off out, dear?

BERYL.

Lady Ripstow and Lord Lurgashall are coming for me at eleven, to take me to see Burne-Jones's pictures.

MRS. BOMPAS.

You haven't kissed me, Beryl.

BERYL.

[*Kissing her forehead.*] I forgot.

MRS. BOMPAS.

[*To herself.*] Forgot!

BERYL.

[*Constrainedly.*] How is papa to-day?

MRS. BOMPAS.

I've not seen him yet. The House sat late and he slept in his dressing-room, to avoid disturbing me. How unkind you are to all of us, Beryl!

BERYL.

I can't help it.

MRS. BOMPAS.

And how rude you were to Mrs. Mountrafford and Miss Mountrafford at Lady Cleaver's party last night.

BERYL.

Mrs. Mountrafford! You mean Mrs. Hooley!

MRS. BOMPAS.

Hush!

BERYL.

Miss Mountrafford! My brother Howard's wife!

MRS. BOMPAS.

Be quiet!

BERYL.

I feel I can't remain quiet! I have an impulse to rush on to the balcony, or on to the doorstep, and cry out to the passers-by, " Look here, this is a house of imposture!"

MRS. BOMPAS.

Don't shout like that!

BERYL.

And when Denham calls—Denham, who believes so in my truthfulness—I am in danger of looking straight into his eyes and saying " Denham, Howard is married—married—and this is the house which contains his young wife and Mrs. Hooley, her silly, simpering mother!"

MRS. BOMPAS.

You'll be heard!

BERYL.

" Yes, yes, yes—this is the house where two humble, ignorant people are dressed up, and made images of, and called Mountrafford, but they are nothing but Hooleys, Hooleys, Hooleys!"

Mrs. Bompas.

You'll drive me distracted! I shan't be able to struggle through the season!

Beryl.

[*Picking up a newspaper.*] More of it! Have you seen this?

Mrs. Bompas.

No—yes—I don't know—of course I have.

Beryl.

One of the "High Life" paragraphs in this week's *Womankind.* [*Reading.*] "The elements of romance are certainly not wanting in connection with the approaching marriage of Mr. Howard Egerton-Bompas, the son of the popular member for St. Swithin's, and the wealthy Miss Corisande Shafto Honoria Mountrafford, whose advent with her delightful mother has already done much to interest and charm society." How awful!

Mrs. Bompas.

Monty—Mr. Trimble—made these people Mountraffords. It has been considered advisable. It is scarcely for women like ourselves to question the wisdom of men like papa and Monty Trimble.

Beryl.

[*Reading.*] "We can only hope that Mrs. Mountrafford will some day find leisure to publish a brief history of her extraordinary missionary labours among the American aborigines."

Mrs. Bompas.

We were obliged to account for her past in a

creditable way. We have been guided solely by Monty.

BERYL.

[*Reading.*] " Surely even the varied pages of fiction present nothing more fascinating than the picture of this philanthropic widow-lady and her fair-haired daughter dwelling for years in almost intimate association with the rude remnants of the scattered Indian tribes."

MRS. BOMPAS.

D-d-don't, Beryl, don't.

BERYL.

I will !

MRS. BOMPAS.

Hush ! Here she is.

BERYL.

Mrs. Hooley !

MRS. BOMPAS.

No—Mountrafford.

BERYL.

Hooley.

MRS. BOMPAS.

Mountrafford !

BERYL.

[*Flourishing the journal.*] Hooley, Hooley, Hooley !

MRS. HOOLEY *and* HONORIA, *both fashionably dressed, enter the room.*

MRS. HOOLEY.

Good morning, Mrs. Egerton-Bompas – good morning, Beryl dear. Did you fear you'd never see us this beautiful morning? Oh, the fascinating party last night!

HONORIA.

[*Speaking with her mouth full of sweetmeats.*] Good morning. Will you taste my pralines?

[MRS. BOMPAS *and* BERYL *decline.*

MRS. HOOLEY.

[*Posing.*] I'm anxious for your opinion on my new frock. My maid declares it's Honoria's sister I'll get taken for.

MRS. BOMPAS.

I'm afraid the woman means the gown is too youthful for you.

MRS. HOOLEY.

And why should I have years put on me when I'm just commencing to enjoy life? Do you fancy I require taking-in anywhere?

[MRS. BOMPAS *arranges* MRS. HOOLEY's *dress.*

HONORIA.

[*To* BERYL.] Another day, and you'll not be good friends with me?

BERYL.

I want to be friends with you, very badly—only friendship must be founded on mutual respect, mustn't it?

HONORIA.

No, must it? [*Popping a sweetmeat into her mouth.*] Sure, I don't know.

BERYL.

Of course it must. And how can we respect each other ?

HONORIA.

And why not, will you tell me ?

BERYL.

Why, you couldn't respect a girl you found telling a—a lie, could you?

HONORIA.

Oh, yes, I could, if I liked her well enough.

BERYL.

Ah, you'll never see things rightly! [*Showing her the newspaper.*] Look there! you couldn't be good friends with a girl who lived and acted *all that,* could you ?

HONORIA.

Oh, mother darling, here's more about us—here's more about us !

[MRS. HOOLEY and HONORIA *read the paper together.*

MRS. HOOLEY.

Ah, look at this now! Oh, the complimentary allusions !

HONORIA.

See here, mother ! Oh, the flattering comments !

JELF *enters, and at the same moment a few chords on a piano in another room are heard.*

MRS. BOMPAS.

What's that ?

JELF.

Mrs. Cormanti and her young lady assistants are here, ma'am. [*He goes out.*

MRS. BOMPAS.

The dancing-mistress, in the coral drawing-room!

MRS. HOOLEY.

Sure, we're taking our lessons there now because of the beautiful floor. Do you mind what follows the waltz this morning, Honoria, darling?

HONORIA.

I do, mother—the Dance of the Sylphs.

MRS. BOMPAS.

The Dance of the Sylphs!

MRS. HOOLEY.

It's an elegant *pas de doo*—for two people—Honoria and me!

MRS. BOMPAS.

You!

MRS. HOOLEY.

And why not? It'll be wanted during the season, Madame Cormanti says, for the cause of some blessed charity. [*The piano is heard again.*] We're coming, Madame Cormanti dear, we're coming!

[MRS. HOOLEY *and* HONORIA *leave the room.*

BERYL.

Oh, mamma, mamma!

[JELF *appears at the door.*

JELF.

Mr. Trimble is coming upstairs, ma'am.

BERYL.

How I detest that man !
[*She goes out, as* TRIMBLE *enters gaily.*

TRIMBLE.

Aha, dear Mrs. E-B !

MRS. BOMPAS.

I *am* glad you're in town again.

TRIMBLE.

My poor dear brother is so much better that I was
able to get back last night, just in time to pop in to
Lady Cleaver's. It cheered me to meet you all there ;
ah, the anxiety of nursing the sick—terrible ! Dear
E-B not visible yet, I hear.

MRS. BOMPAS.

No.

TRIMBLE.

And our new dear friends, Mrs.—ah—Mountrafford
and Miss Mountrafford—what progress have they
made in the arts and graces while I've been away?
Are we putting the finishing touches, h'm ?

[*The air of a waltz is heard.*

MRS. BOMPAS.

They are taking their dancing-lesson now.

TRIMBLE.

Good. And the younger lady's French—we are
helping her with a few indispensable phrases ?

E

MRS. BOMPAS.

Ah, I was, obliged to pack off the French governess in a hurry.

TRIMBLE.

Why?

MRS. BOMPAS.

She pried too much.

TRIMBLE.

H'm, dangerous. Get somebody else.

MRS. BOMPAS.

I've engaged Miss Tuck, Kate Cazalet's little niece.

TRIMBLE.

The relative of a friend—is that quite judicious?

MRS. BOMPAS.

The poor girl always has a headache, and seems too spiritless to be inquisitive.

TRIMBLE.

Well, well, then everything is going on charmingly. [*Eating a lozenge.*] Really, I am not a sentimental man, but I *do* think we ought to feel profoundly grateful.

MRS. BOMPAS.

Grateful?

TRIMBLE.

When we consider how eminently presentable these dear people are. I watched them at Lady Cleaver's last night, and I felt proud of my small share in improving their condition in life, honestly proud. Yes, dear friend, let us feel deeply grateful, unreservedly happy.

MRS. BOMPAS.

Monty—— !

TRIMBLE.

You're not worried about anything surely !

MRS. BOMPAS.

Yes, there's something I'm keeping from Percy.

TRIMBLE.

Keeping from him ?

MRS. BOMPAS.

Well, haven't told him. His temper has become so ungovernable since our misfortune that I'm almost frightened to tell him. Here ! Monty—Heaven forgive me for my vulgarity !—but this confounded Irish widow has actually picked up a sweetheart.

TRIMBLE.

No ! Why didn't you write to me ? Has it gone far ?

MRS. BOMPAS.

He's after her every hour of the day; he left a note here yesterday—*here*, with some flowers.

TRIMBLE.

Who's the beast ?

MRS. BOMPAS.

Why, the creature my husband hates of all men in the world; that's the reason I've held my tongue, hoping I was wrong in my conclusions.

TRIMBLE.

Well, but who, who, who?

MRS. BOMPAS.

The little reptile who ridicules Percy in the House, the member for Ballymara.

TRIMBLE.

Mr. McShane!

MRS. BOMPAS.

Timothy McShane.

TRIMBLE.

Damn! Ah, excuse my breach of manners—I haven't sworn for years.

MRS. BOMPAS.

Sit down.

TRIMBLE.

Dear Mrs. E-B!

MRS. BOMPAS.

The silly woman met him first at Mrs. Shekleton's crush, the night Honoria made her *début* as Miss Mountrafford. Of course, after all, she's only eight-and-thirty, and she wore one of my diamond necklaces.

TRIMBLE.

I know—I know.

MRS. BOMPAS.

Well, the Sunday following I fell over them with their heads together at Church Parade. And this last week I've seen them everywhere—picture-galleries—shops——

TRIMBLE.

Bless my soul!

MRS. BOMPAS.

And, if they are really in love, don't you realise the volcano we're all sitting upon?

TRIMBLE.

I certainly perceive——

MRS. BOMPAS.

That she's a weak-brained, vain creature with no prudence, no—no——

TRIMBLE.

No invention!

MRS. BOMPAS.

And suppose the fool of a man proposes to her?

TRIMBLE.

Why, you don't apprehend——!

MRS. BOMPAS.

Suppose in a moment of middle-aged emotion she confided in him.

TRIMBLE.

Confided?

MRS. BOMPAS.

Our secret.

TRIMBLE.

Oh!

MRS. BOMPAS.

She couldn't marry without doing so. Monty, in mercy's name, shut your mouth and collect yourself!

TRIMBLE.

My dear Mrs. E-B, I—I frankly, I—I candidly admit this is a contingency which even I did not anticipate.

JELF *enters, carrying a large basket of flowers.*

JELF.

For Mrs. Mountrafford, ma'am.

MRS. BOMPAS.

Stop! D-d-don't disturb Mrs. Mountrafford now. P-put it down.

> [JELF *deposits the basket on the table and goes out.*

MRS. BOMPAS.

What did I tell you!

TRIMBLE.

His card is attached to it.

MRS. BOMPAS.

I saw that.

TRIMBLE.

[*Reading card.*] " Mr. Timothy McShane." A message, in pencil.

MRS. BOMPAS.

I thought so. Read it!

TRIMBLE.

Forgive me, dear Mrs. E-B—certain things I cannot do.

> [*He hands the basket to* MRS. BOMPAS ; *she reads the message.*

Mrs. Bompas.

Ah !

Trimble.

Pray relieve my anxiety.

Mrs. Bompas.

" Shall present myself in the course of the day to settle matters."

Trimble.

This gentleman is unmistakably serious in his intentions.

Mrs. Bompas.

Advise me.

Trimble.

Dear E-B must put his foot down at once.

Mrs. Bompas.

Yes, yes. But what a scene there will be ! Who is to tell him. Monty, will you ?

Trimble.

No, no—you break the ice. I must not be suspected of a desire to unduly intrude.

[JELF *appears.*

Jelf.

Miss Cazalet—Miss Tuck. ·

Mrs. Bompas.

Bother the people—at this moment !

[MISS CAZALET *enters with* LUCY TUCK
JELF *withdraws.*

MISS CAZALET.

[*Kissing* MRS. BOMPAS.] Dear Mrs. Egerton-Bompas!

MRS. BOMPAS.

So pleased to see you.

MISS CAZALET.

I've brought my little mouse. How d'ye do, Mr. Trimble?

TRIMBLE.

We meet too seldom.

LUCY.

[*To* MRS. BOMPAS.] I will do my best to be service-able to you and Miss—Miss—Mountrafford, is it?

MRS. BOMPAS.

Y-yes, Mountrafford.

LUCY.

Ah, you don't know how much it means to me to feel independent.

MRS. BOMPAS.

Child!

LUCY.

I—I mean, to feel myself not a burden upon—upon my—my—my aunt.

MRS. BOMPAS.

I'll call Honoria. [*She opens the door.*] Honoria! Oh, that ridiculous old woman! The dance of the Sylphs! Stop!

[*She goes out, and the music ceases.*

MISS CAZALET.

[*To* TRIMBLE.] Now it's truly friendly of you to ask after the *Morning Message*.

TRIMBLE.

One of the most valuable newspapers in London, *I* consider.

MISS CAZALET.

You know I call it my poor, ailing, rickety baby. Well, the *Morning Message* is—teething. It may outlive its infantile complaints——

TRIMBLE.

It must.

MISS CAZALET. ·

But, oh, people won't advertise as much as a lost dog in it. And then, I have such trouble with its nurses—I mean, its editors.

TRIMBLE.

[*Smothering a yawn.*] I'm profoundly sorry.

MISS CAZALET.

The first was knocked down by a four-wheeler, and is now contributing a depressing series of articles called " Happy Hospitals." The second departed abruptly last night.

TRIMBLE.

Ill ?

MISS CAZALET.

Heartbroken ; wanted to marry—you know whom. And I'm left with a sub-editor with a large head and limited experience. Oh ! All my life I've tired of a new toy after a fortnight, and I've been the real live proprietress of this influential journal for a whole month! Ugh!

HONORIA *enters with* MRS. BOMPAS.

MISS CAZALET.

[*Kissing* HONORIA.] My dear Miss Mountrafford.

[LUCY *and* HONORIA *shake hands.*

HONORIA.

[*To* LUCY.] I'm glad you've come.

LUCY.

Oh, thank you.

HONORIA.

[*Confidentially.*] We'll have a fine time of it if you'll not bother me with your instruction. Have a praline?

MRS. BOMPAS.

Honoria, take Miss Tuck upstairs yourself, and make her feel at home.

HONORIA.

I'll do that.

[HONORIA *and* LUCY *go out.*

MISS CAZALET.

Let me see my little mouse's gilded cage—may I?

[*She follows* HONORIA *and* LUCY.

MRS. BOMPAS.

Oh! all these people! [*To* TRIMBLE.] Monty, Monty, find out if Percy is in the library yet; if so, tell him I must speak to him at once, at once.

TRIMBLE.

Bless me, yes—at once.   Dear Mrs. E-B——

MRS. BOMPAS.

What now !

TRIMBLE.

H'm, I don't think I should make such a very close friend of Miss Cazalet.

MRS. BOMPAS.

She makes herself a friend.

TRIMBLE.

I should check it.   I always recommend that friendships should be regulated with a view to future disagreements.

MRS. BOMPAS.

But we are not going to disagree.

TRIMBLE.

I hope not ; I'm sure she's not a person one would derive any pleasure from offending.

MRS. BOMPAS.

Oh, try and find Percy !

TRIMBLE.

Ah, dear E-B.

[*He goes out, as* JELF *appears at the door.*

JELF.

Lady Ripstow and Lord Lurgashall are waiting for Miss Beryl in their carriage, ma'am.

MRS. BOMPAS.

I'll find Miss Beryl and bring her downstairs.

[*She goes out quickly.*

JELF.

[*At the door.*] I wasn't aware that your ladyship was coming up.

LADY RIPSTOW *and* DENHAM *enter.* JELF *withdraws.*

LADY RIPSTOW.

Yes, Denham, I have indeed observed a serious change in Beryl.

DENHAM.

It worries me dreadfully, mother.

LADY RIPSTOW.

A coolness of manner——

DENHAM.

Towards myself.

LADY RIPSTOW.

Even to me.   An abruptness of speech——

DENHAM.

To both of us.

LADY RIPSTOW.

Followed by a suffusion of the eyes.

DENHAM.

For the life of me, I can't guess the reason.

LADY RIPSTOW.

Ah, but *I* can.

DENHAM.

Mother!

LADY RIPSTOW.

Unless I am gravely mistaken, the pardonable cause
of Beryl's distress of mind is—will you hear it?

DENHAM.

Go on.

LADY RIPSTOW.

It is that, notwithstanding all the diplomatic
advances of the Egerton-Bompases, your father has
never called.

DENHAM.

Bah!

LADY RIPSTOW.

Denham!

*MISS CAZALET enters, and is momentarily discon-
certed at seeing* LADY RIPSTOW *and* DENHAM.

MISS CAZALET.

Oh, how d'ye do? And how do *you* do, Lady Ripstow?

LADY RIPSTOW.

Miss Cazalet!

MISS CAZALET.

And how is Lord Ripstow?

DENHAM.

[*Placing himself between* LADY RIPSTOW *and* MISS
CAZALET.] In spite of advancing years Lord Ripstow
has only one infirmity, Miss Cazalet.

MISS CAZALET.

Only one *now?* And that —— ?

DENHAM.

The infirmity of forgetting certain former acquaintances.

MISS CAZALET.

Or of brooding over them. Poor old age!

LADY RIPSTOW.

[*To* DENHAM.] The second time this has occurred!

DENHAM.

I hear, her niece——

LADY RIPSTOW.

Before to-day is over Mrs. Egerton-Bompas shall know that if that woman is received here I will never enter this house again: she shall choose between me and Miss Cazalet.

MRS. BOMPAS *and* BERYL *enter.*

MRS. BOMPAS.

Oh, my dear Lady Ripstow—Lord Lurgashall! Beryl!

BOMPAS, *who is very excited, enters, followed by* TRIMBLE.

BOMPAS.

[*Kissing* BERYL.] Hah, Berry, my dear, I've some wonderful news for you. Eh? Oh! How d'ye do, how d'ye do, how d'ye do? Glad you're all here—I've good news for everybody. Aha, what d'ye think, what d'ye think? Guess now, guess, guess!

MRS. BOMPAS.

Hush! Percy, what is it?

BOMPAS.

My chance has come!

MRS. BOMPAS.

Chance?

BOMPAS.

Why, a great compliment has been paid me—an enormous compliment. To-night, you know, finishes this big full-dress debate on the Irish Question, and the Whips have asked me to speak.

MRS. BOMPAS.

Oh, Percy!

BOMPAS.

To speak! [*To* DENHAM *and* LADY RIPSTOW, *shaking hands with them suddenly.*] I didn't shake hands, did I? Excuse me. [*Addressing all.*] There have been people who've said "Egerton-Bompas will never do anything in the House." "Won't he!" I've thought. "Once in, he'll never open his mouth"—thousands have said that. Ha, ha, ha! [*Shaking hands with* MISS CAZALET.] Did I shake hands? My head's so full of my speech; it isn't that success alters me at all. Here, you'll all want to come down to the House to-night, of course?

LADY RIPSTOW.

I fear——

BOMPAS.

Oh, I can manage it—there's nothing I can't manage. I've got seats in the ladies' gallery, and another man will give me his. That'll be two Egerton-Bompases, one Ripstow, one Cazalet——

MISS CAZALET.

At what time are you likely to speak?

BOMPAS.

About nine o'clock.

MISS CAZALET.

H'm, during the dinner-hour, isn't it?

BOMPAS.

Yes. [*Struck by the look on* MISS CAZALET's *face.*]
Oh! Well, some men—like—speaking—during the
dinner-hour. Eh?

MISS CAZALET.

Delightful—such freedom from interruption. [*To*
MRS. BOMPAS.] Send word to Boswell Court, dear,
when and where I'm to join you—wire " Feverheat,
London." Don't stir! Good-bye, all! Or telephone,
3033. Lady Ripstow! [*She goes out.*

BOMPAS.

[*To* LADY RIPSTOW.] I've the notes of my speech
in the library; I've been up half the night over it.
I expect you'd like to hear——

LADY RIPSTOW.

Pray excuse me this morning. Lurgashall, are
you ready?

BOMPAS.

Going out, Berry? Proud of your father, hey?
Proud of him?

BERYL.

Oh, papa!

TRIMBLE.

May I put Lady Ripstow into her carriage?
[*To* MRS. BOMPAS.] Your opportunity.

> [LADY RIPSTOW *and* TRIMBLE *go out.*

BOMPAS.

[*Slapping* DENHAM *on the back as he passes.*] Lucky
dog!

MRS. BOMPAS.

Good-bye, children.

> [BERYL *and* DENHAM *leave the room
> together.*

MRS. BOMPAS.

Now!

BOMPAS.

Clara! Aha, old lady, give me a kiss. [*She kisses
him.*] So, they've found me out at last, hey?

MRS. BOMPAS.

Found you out?

BOMPAS.

Found out my value. This is a gigantic opportunity—by Jove, it is! Nice flowers you've got here.

MRS. BOMPAS.

Percy dear——

BOMPAS.

First of all, Clara, I mean to let that little beast
McShane have it—straight from the shoulder.

MRS. BOMPAS.

Percy, I—I want to——

F

Bompas.

[*Selecting a rose and putting it in his buttonhole.*]
Who sent you these? Lovely perfume. Straight
from the shoulder! Mr. Timothy McShane hasn't
nicknamed me " Blankets " for nothing. Blankets !

Mrs. Bompas.

Percy !

Bompas.

Eh? [*Turning the basket of flowers about.*] I'm
looking for a bit of green.

Mrs. Bompas.

I've something to tell you that may—put you out.

Bompas.

Ha, ha ! Things are going too well for that, old
lady. What is it, a big cheque, or a——? [*Reading
the card attached to the basket.*] " Mr. Timothy
McShane." Mr.—Timothy—McShane. Clara?

Mrs. Bompas.

Mr. McShane left that, or sent it.

Bompas.

The coward ! The—the worm ! So he guesses I
mean to have a slap at him to-night, does he ? And he
thinks to quiet me by sending you—a few—
paltry——!

> [*He tears the flower from his coat and is
> about to attack the basket.*

Mrs. Bompas.

No, no, they're not sent to me.

BOMPAS.

What d'ye mean?

MRS. BOMPAS.

They're—Mrs. Mountrafford's.

BOMPAS.

Eh?

MRS. BOMPAS.

Read the other side.

BOMPAS.

[*Reading.*] " Shall present myself in the course of the day to settle matters." W-what matters?

MRS. BOMPAS.

L-l-love matters. He has—fallen in love—with—Mrs. Mountrafford. Percy!

BOMPAS.

[*In a rage.*] What's been going on?

MRS. BOMPAS.

Nothing—not much. They were introduced to each other at Mrs. Shekleton's. Since then—they've met—here and there—occasionally. I didn't attach much importance to it at first; I tried not to, knowing how the very name of McShane infuriates you. But now the matter—has grown—too serious——

BOMPAS.

Serious! serious!

MRS. BOMPAS.

Yes, yes, because you see, Percy—you see——

BOMPAS.

See! What?

MRS. BOMPAS.

That if he proposes to her, as he evidently means
to——

BOMPAS.

Marriage!

MRS. BOMPAS.

Of course, marriage. Then, Percy—Percy! then
she would either have to refuse him or to—to—tell
him!

BOMPAS.

To tell him—tell him! Ahhh!

MRS. BOMPAS.

Percy, you mustn't give way to these uncontrollable fits of anger! We—we never calculated for
this. We forgot she's not at all a bad-looking
woman——

BOMPAS.

Cat! I hate her! A simpering cat!

MRS. BOMPAS.

We mustn't be upset by this—this trifle. We
must send for her and—coax her——

BOMPAS.

Coax her! Cat!

MRS. BOMPAS.

And when Mr. McShane calls——

BOMPAS.

I—I could see him strangled on the floor of the

House! I could! And he—dares to—to come after my widow!

MRS. BOMPAS.

Not your widow.

BOMPAS.

She's ours, body and boots. We've bought her. *I've* bought her,—and paid for her!

MRS. BOMPAS.

Not so loud!

BOMPAS.

And now she'd get me into a mess, would she! She'd expose me, would she, me and **my** family! She'd ruin me! Ruin me!

MRS. BOMPAS.

Percy, these rages are dreadful!

BOMPAS.

Old Mother Hooley! Cat!

MRS. BOMPAS.

You who declare you'll some day attain the highest position—you'll never do it with such a temper!

BOMPAS.

Won't I! Won't I! You'll see if I don't! You'll—— !

MRS. BOMPAS.

There, there—hush, hush! You're all of a tremble.

BOMPAS.

McShane! Blankets!

Mrs. Bompas.

Sit down, darling, and talk it over with Clara. That's right—that's right!

> [*He sinks on to the settee in a heap.*

Mrs. Bompas.

Now you're yourself again, aren't you?

Bompas.

McShane and our—cat!

Mrs. Bompas.

We'll soon put matters straight—you and I, old man—you and I.

Trimble enters quietly.

Trimble.

[*To* Mrs. Bompas, *in a whisper.*] Well?

Mrs. Bompas.

He's had one.

Trimble.

Bad?

Mrs. Bompas.

Shocking! Percy darling—here's Monty.

[Bompas *raises himself slowly and looks at* Trimble.

Trimble.

[*Taking a lozenge.*] H'm, this has rather upset you, dear E-B.

Bompas.

No—not very well—overwork. What's got to be done—about this? What's—got—to be——?

TRIMBLE.

Dear friend, there's not the remotest cause for discomposure. In the first place, allow me to ring the bell.

MRS. BOMPAS.

[*Smiling at* BOMPAS *encouragingly.*] Monty is so useful.

TRIMBLE.

Having summoned the servant, I suggest you give instructions that everybody is distinctly out to Mr. McShane.

MRS. BOMPAS.

Out.

BOMPAS.

Out. [JELF *appears.*] Look here! If a man named McShane presumes to shew his——

MRS. BOMPAS.

Percy!

TRIMBLE.

Jelf, if Mr. McShane calls—you know him?

JELF.

Short gentleman, with flowers, sir.

BOMPAS.

Short——!

MRS. BOMPAS.

Hush!

TRIMBLE

You are quite right—out. No matter whom he inquires for—out.

MRS. BOMPAS.

Out.

BOMPAS.

Out.

JELF.

Not at home, sir.   [JELF *withdraws.*

BOMPAS.

I've done that!

TRIMBLE.

Now, all you have to do further is to see Mrs.
Mountrafford— .

BOMPAS.

Cat!

TRIMBLE.

And, in a few well-chosen, temperate words, inform
her that this sort of thing emphatically will not do.

[*The music is heard again.*

BOMPAS.

What's that?

MRS. BOMPAS.

She is taking her dancing-lesson——

[BOMPAS *makes excitedly for the door.*

TRIMBLE.

[*Stopping him.*] No, no, dear E-B, you must
pledge your word that you will conduct this interview in a reasonable, moderate——

MRS. BOMPAS.

Statesmanlike——

TRIMBLE.

Statesmanlike fashion. Certainly, statesmanlike.

BOMPAS.

Statesmanlike ?   I understand.   You shall see.

TRIMBLE.

Good !

BOMPAS.

[*To* MRS. BOMPAS.]   You said my temper would keep me from attaining a big position !

MRS. BOMPAS.

Yes, but——

BOMPAS.

You did !   Well, you'll see whether I can command myself.

TRIMBLE.

That's right, dear E-B !

BOMPAS.

Bring her in, Monty.   Percy Egerton-Bompas has no dignity, no self-restraint, hasn't he !   I'll show you.

TRIMBLE.

[*Opening the door and calling.*]   Good morning, dear Mrs. Mountrafford.   Ah, you almost tripped !

[*The music stops abruptly, and* MRS. HOOLEY *appears in the doorway.*]

MRS. HOOLEY.

[*Breathlessly.*]   Oh, Mr. Trimble !   Oh, the intoxication of the dance !

[TRIMBLE *goes out.*

MRS. HOOLEY.

It's one trifling movement I'll never conquer.

" One—two—three—and—four. Sure, the "and—
four," will break the heart of me.

[TRIMBLE *returns.*

TRIMBLE.

[*To* BOMPAS.] I've dismissed Cormanti.

MRS. HOOLEY.

[*Practising.*] One—two—three—and—and——

BOMPAS.

Be seated, ma'am.

MRS. HOOLEY.

Ah! The turn you gave me!

BOMPAS.

Mrs. Everard Shafto Mountrafford!

MRS. HOOLEY.

Yes?

BOMPAS.

A basket of flowers has been left for you at my
door——

MRS. HOOLEY.

A bookay!

BOMPAS.

This basket of—— Where is it? Where is it?

MRS. BOMPAS.

All right, dear—here.

[*She pushes the basket from beneath the table,
where she had concealed it.*

TRIMBLE.

Here.

BOMPAS.

[*Snatching the basket.*] It's thrown me out—thrown me out.

MRS. BOMPAS.

[*Quietly to* BOMPAS.] No, no—capital, Percy.

TRIMBLE.

Excellent beginning, dear friend.

BOMPAS.

Attached to this basket, Mrs. Mountrafford, I find a card.

[*He looks vainly for the card, which has been left in* TRIMBLE'S *hand.*

TRIMBLE.

Certainly, a card.

MRS. HOOLEY.

A card !

BOMPAS.

Where's the thing gone to ?   Where is it ?

TRIMBLE.

Are you looking for the card, E-B ?

BOMPAS.

[*Grabbing the card from* TRIMBLE *who is smoothing it out.*] Looking for the——!

MRS. BOMPAS.

Percy !

TRIMBLE.

Dear friend !

BOMPAS.

Er—the—ah—if—when—— Thrown out completely !

TRIMBLE.

[*In a whisper.*] Hand it to her.

BOMPAS.

Leave me alone. [*Giving the basket to* MRS.
HOOLEY.] There, ma'am.

MRS. HOOLEY.

My card !

BOMPAS.

Take it !

MRS. HOOLEY.

[*Reading the card.*] Oh, look at this now !   Oh the
politeness of it !   Oh, the——!

BOMPAS.

[*Silencing* TRIMBLE *and* MRS. BOMPAS.]   Don't
interfere ! [*To* MRS. HOOLEY.]   So, ma'am, so, Mrs.
Mountrafford, this is the return you make me, *me*,
ME !

MRS. HOOLEY.

And I should like to know, Mr. Egerton-Bompas,
what you've got to complain of !

BOMPAS.

Complain of !   Who has rescued you from—from
obscure poverty, ma'am, you and your—your brat !

MRS. BOMPAS.

Percy !

TRIMBLE.

E-B !

BOMPAS.

Silence !   Who has received you into his domestic

circle, his sacred domestic circle ? Who has placed you upon a social level with his own family, mercifully thrown the—the—the veil of oblivion over your humble origin, and opened to you the—the—the gates of the most exclusive society in the world !

MRS. BOMPAS.

Quite so, dear.

TRIMBLE.

This is admirable.

BOMPAS.

Who, placing his son's happiness above every other consideration, has consented to an alliance between that son and your daughter ? Who——— ?

MRS. HOOLEY.

And indeed, Mr. Egerton-Bompas, sir, I'm not an ungrateful lady.

BOMPAS.

Show it, prove it !

MRS. HOOLEY.

But I confess I'm not unwilling to relieve you of the burden of my keep and clothing.

BOMPAS.

I don't want you to relieve me of it ! I've got you ! I—I carry you upon my shoulders for as long as you choose to live !

MRS. BOMPAS.

Woman, you don't understand ! You couldn't marry now without—without———

TRIMBLE.

Without entering into a long and painful explana-
tion.

MRS. HOOLEY.

Philoo! I'd explain everything in five minutes.

MRS. BOMPAS and TRIMBLE.

No!

BOMPAS.

Where's your refinement—where's your womanly
feeling—where's your sense of shame?

[*They gather round* MRS. HOOLEY, *protesting
excitedly.*

MRS. HOOLEY.

Have done! Don't bustle me!

[*She breaks away from them, pursued by*
MRS. BOMPAS.

BOMPAS.

[*To* TRIMBLE.] Well? Well?

TRIMBLE.

Dear friend, I—I frankly, I—I candidly admit
that this is a complication which even I——

HOWARD *enters, in riding dress, with a tradesman's
account in his hand.*

HOWARD.

Morning, morning! Jolly in the Park this morning.

BOMPAS.

[*Turning upon him furiously.*] Jolly in the Park!

HOWARD.

There! At me again! A nice time I've had of it this last month! Didn't you say I might come to you to-day for a cheque for my florist?

BOMPAS.

Get out of my sight!

[Mrs. BOMPAS *and* TRIMBLE *lead* HOWARD *towards the door.*

HOWARD.

When *do* I do right? I dun' know!

BOMPAS.

Bah!

HOWARD.

I s'pose I may mention there's somebody waiting to see you in the library.

BOMPAS.

Where the notes of my speech are lying about!

MRS. BOMPAS.

Who puts a visitor there?

HOWARD.

At me again! Why, when I let myself in just now I found a man on the doorstep who wanted to see pa particularly.

TRIMBLE.

Ah! what name, dear young friend?

HOWARD.

McShane. [BOMPAS, TRIMBLE, *and* MRS BOMPAS, *stand transfixed with horror.*] What *now?*

MRS. HOOLEY.

Did you say Mr. McShane? Ah, he's called to see my trustee.

TRIMBLE.

Your trustee?

MRS. HOOLEY.

Well, he asked if Mr. Egerton-Bompas was my trustee. Sure, what was I to say, situated as I am?

MRS. BOMPAS.

[*To* HOWARD.] Get the notes of your father's speech from his table. You'll break our hearts.

HOWARD.

Wrong again! 　　　　　　　　[*He goes out.*

MRS. HOOLEY.

I'll retire to my room while the delicate interview takes place. Am I to understand that obstacles are to be thrown in our path?

BOMPAS.

[*To himself.*] In my house—Blankets!

TRIMBLE.

[*To* MRS. HOOLEY.] Everything shall be done that gentlemen can do to protect the interests of a lady whose welfare they have at heart. 　　[*She goes out.*

MRS. BOMPAS.

Percy! Be—be—be statesmanlike!

BOMPAS.

Go after her! Keep your eye on her! Don't
leave her!

MRS. BOMPAS.

Yes, yes. Oh, my poor Percy!
[*She leaves them,* TRIMBLE *rings the bell.*

BOMPAS.

Well? well?

TRIMBLE.

Dear friend, I—I frankly, I—I candidly admit
that this particular complication is one which even I
——Eh?

JELF enters.

TRIMBLE.

Mr. McShane is in the library?

JELF.

In the library, sir.

TRIMBLE.

Show him up.

[JELF *retires.* TRIMBLE *nervously turns the
key in the doors, leaving only one un-
locked.*

BOMPAS.

Monty?

TRIMBLE.

You must be secured from interruption.

G

BOMPAS.

What—what's our attitude, our policy?

TRIMBLE.

To keep them apart for the next few hours. To-morrow we must get this ill-bred woman out of England, somehow. Really, I—I'm quite upset.

BOMPAS.

Stand by me, Monty, when the—the lies are wanted.

TRIMBLE.

[*Taking a lozenge.*] Command me—command me.

BOMPAS.

Monty, don't you think that in the highest social and political circles a man, even to maintain his position, may tell one lie too many?

TRIMBLE.

Hush! Dear friend, no one deplores a falsehood more than myself, but, let us always remember, the demand creates the supply.

BOMPAS.

But isn't there—one special moment—in a man's life when he'd better—resist the demand?

TRIMBLE.

Resist?

BOMPAS.

Y—y—yes.

TRIMBLE.

Oh, my dear E-B, in my own experience, there

is more time wasted in resisting temptation than
over anything in this world.   Hark!

JELF *shows in* MR. TIMOTHY MCSHANE, *a smartly
dressed, eager, dark little man of forty-five or
fifty, with a pale face, restless eyes, and a high
forehead.   He carries an umbrella aggressively.*

MCSHANE.

Mr. Egerton-Bompas.

BOMPAS.

Mr. McShane.

MCSHANE.

[*Looking at* TRIMBLE.] Mr. ——

BOMPAS.

Mr. Montague Trimble, my friend and confidential
adviser.

TRIMBLE.

How dy'e do?   What delightful weather we're——

BOMPAS.

[*To* MCSHANE.] Be seated.

[TRIMBLE *quietly locks the door.*

MCSHANE.

Mr. Bompas, your political convictions and my own
are as wide asunder as the poles. [BOMPAS *bows.*]
That is, so far as I have been privileged to gather;
for hitherto your individual public policy has been
one of intense, ardent silence.

BOMPAS.

To-night, Mr. McShane, that silence is to be broken.
To-night——

McShane.

Sir, I can promise you at least one auditor.

Bompas.

I thank you.

McShane.

But, Mr. Bompas, apart from our political divergence, I've noticed that there has crept insidiously into our personal relations a rancorous animosity.

Bompas.

On more than one occasion you have thought it—ah—decent to taunt me with my honourable association with—ah—er—a branch of commerce——

McShane.

Blankets ?

Bompas.

I do not blush to repeat the word ' blankets.'

McShane.

Mr. Bompas, a moment has arrived when private differences must be suspended, antipathies softened. It is the first time in my life I've made such a suggestion to mortal man, but the circumstances are exceptional. Mr. Bompas, I have been fortunate enough to win the affections of the sweet lady who now compliments you by sheltering under your roof, of whose worldly interests I believe you are the legal supervisor.

Bompas.

Sir, you allude, I think, to——?

McShane.

Mrs. Everard Shafto Mountrafford—Kathleen. Mr.

Bompas, to better enable me to pay such prolonged attentions to this charming lady as duty and inclination demand, and to give me the opportunity of entering freely this morning into the subject of the settlement of her pecuniary estate, I suggest there should prevail between you and me, in our private relations, peace. Peace—temporary or permanent! Perhaps it would be more convenient to both of us if we said temporary.

[BOMPAS *bows—they shake hands quickly and distrustfully.* MCSHANE *then puts down his umbrella.*

McSHANE.

And now, sir, as Mrs. Mountrafford is not in her minority, I propose that she be invited to join this agreeable meeting.

BOMPAS.

Eh? No, sir—out of the question.

McSHANE.

Sir!

BOMPAS.

She has expressed a desire—ah—not to be present.

McSHANE.

Tssh, tssh, tssh! Kathleen will waive that objection.

BOMPAS.

Mr. McShane, I—I—er—allow me to consult my friend. [*To* TRIMBLE.] Eh? Eh? [*They whisper together.*] Mr. McShane, you force me to acquaint you with a circumstance which I would willingly have

kept from you. Mrs. Mountrafford is—suddenly—
indisposed.

McShane.

Powers! What is it?

Bompas.

The doctor hasn't seen her yet, but—but——

Trimble.

I think I heard dear Mrs. Egerton-Bompas mention the unpleasant word Influenza.

McShane.

You don't tell me that! Oh! and to think of her
as she was but yesterday! Her gaiety! Her flow
of animal spirits! [*Snatching up his umbrella and turning excitedly to* Bompas.] She is in your house, Mr.
Bompas! I warn you, sir! You are answerable for
the welfare of this charming lady!

Bompas.

[*To* Trimble.] Well? Well?

Trimble.

A rude wild beast.

McShane.

I can't, I won't, realise it! This graceful, this
vivacious lady. Is she in bed or out?

[Trimble *and* Bompas *consult together.*

Bompas.

Out!

McShane.

Out!

BOMPAS.

In. In and out.

McSHANE.

Restless?

BOMPAS.

Uneasy.

McSHANE.

[*Shaking his fist close to* BOMPAS'S *face.*] Take care of her, sir! Take care of her!

BOMPAS.

Mr. McShane!

TRIMBLE.

Really!

McSHANE.

Mr. Bompas, I apologise for that gesture. It was uncontrollable. [TRIMBLE *prompts* BOMPAS.

BOMPAS.

Eh? Yes. [*To* McSHANE.] May I suggest that under the circumstances it would hardly be—be——

TRIMBLE.

Chivalrous.

BOMPAS.

Chivalrous to—to——

McSHANE.

Spare your hints, sir. My distress of mind would not permit me to discuss Mrs. Mountrafford's pecuniary affairs while that accomplished, that amiable lady ——There's some one at your door.

[*The door handle is rattled, then a knock is heard.*

BOMPAS.

Whoisit ?

TRIMBLE.

Who—is—it ?

JELF.

[*Outside.*] Jelf, sir—with a note.

TRIMBLE.

Oh, a note.

JELF.

For Mr. McShane, sir.

TRIMBLE.

For Mr. McShane !

JELF.

From Mrs. Mountrafford, sir.

[BOMPAS *and* TRIMBLE *look at each other aghast.*

McSHANE.

May I ask if that servant is ever to be admitted ?

BOMPAS.

Er—I—er——

TRIMBLE.

I—I—pardon me——

[TRIMBLE *takes a letter from* JELF, *then re-locks door.*

McSHANE.

Am I to be allowed to have my letter ?

[TRIMBLE *reluctantly hands the letter to* McSHANE, *who opens it.*

BOMPAS.

[*To* TRIMBLE.] Ass! Ass!

TRIMBLE.

What could I do, E-B?

BOMPAS.

From her to him! Ass!

McSHANE.

[*Reading to himself.*] "Meet me to-day, usual place, same hour. Kathleen."

[*He refolds, and pockets the note.*

BOMPAS.

[*To* TRIMBLE.] What's in it? What's in it?

McSHANE.

Mr. Bompas. I have the honour to wish you Good-morning. [*Extending his hand.*] Temporary.

TRIMBLE.

I'll take Mr. McShane downstairs.

[McSHANE *passes out, and* TRIMBLE *follows.*

BOMPAS.

Oh! What's in it? What's in it? What's in it?

MRS. BOMPAS *enters quickly.*

MRS. BOMPAS.

Percy! I'm mad with anxiety! I've been listening at every door trying to catch a word or two. He's gone! Tell me! Percy! Tell me!

BOMPAS.

Why—why didn't you remain with her ?

MRS. BOMPAS.

There was no necessity. I saw her let her hair down, and begin to write her letters.

BOMPAS.

Yes. She's written one to McShane !

MRS. BOMPAS.

To McShane !

BOMPAS.

And he's got it !

MRS. BOMPAS.

No ! What's in it ?

BOMPAS.

Ah-h-h ! What's in it !

TRIMBLE *enters, agitated.*

BOMPAS.

Well ? Well ?

TRIMBLE.

E-B ! E-B, I have committed an act—for you, dear friend, for you !—which I shall always find it extremely difficult to palliate.

BOMPAS.

What !

MRS. BOMPAS.

Monty !

TRIMBLE.

I—I am ashamed to say [*producing* MRS. HOOLEY'S *note*] that I have picked Mr. McShane's pocket.

BOMPAS.

Here——!

[BOMPAS *snatches the note from* TRIMBLE.

MRS. BOMPAS.

[*Looking over her husband's shoulder.*] Oh!

TRIMBLE.

I have no desire to pry into the contents of a communication addressed to another person; at the same time——

BOMPAS.

[*Reading.*] " Meet me to-day, usual place, same hour."

MRS. BOMPAS.

What place?

BOMPAS.

What hour? Advise me!

TRIMBLE.

[*Ringing bell.*] She mustn't go out, obviously.

MRS. BOMPAS.

The wretch! I'll turn the key of her door! I will! I will! [*She goes out.*

BOMPAS.

Well? Well?

TRIMBLE.

I—I—frankly, I—I candidly admit that this—is
—a——

JELF enters.

TRIMBLE.

Jelf, Mr. Egerton-Bompas's orders are that you
station yourself downstairs at the front door——

BOMPAS.

Yes, yes; you and Chalmers and Hodgson—three
of you!

TRIMBLE.

No, no—Hodgson at the tradesman's door——

BOMPAS.

I said so.

TRIMBLE.

And that from this moment no one shall be allowed
to leave the house till you have first communicated
with him or myself.

BOMPAS.

Understand?

JELF.

Certainly, sir. [JELF *withdraws.*

BOMPAS.

I've done that! I've done that! I've done that!

MRS. BOMPAS totters in.

BOMPAS.

Clara!

Mrs. Bompas.

Percy—she is a double-faced woman! She—let her hair down—to hoodwink me.

Bompas.

Hoodwink!

Mrs. Bompas.

My poor husband! She—she has—gone out.
[*The three are speechless for a moment.*

Bompas.

[*Suddenly catching* Trimble *by the throat.*] Devil! devil!

Trimble.

Dear friend!

Mrs. Bompas.

Percy!

[Bompas *shakes* Mrs. Bompas *off.*

Bompas.

[*To* Trimble.] You tempted me! You have brought this on me! You! [*He releases* Trimble, *who tumbles on to the floor.*] Devil! But for you I should never have done—all I have done! I should have stopped short at a great deal—but for you! And now——! Find this woman! Keep them apart! Bring her home before she meets him! She's mine! I've bought her! Bring her home! Bring her home!

Trimble.

Where am I to look for her, E-B

BOMPAS.

[*Throwing the note at him.*] There!

TRIMBLE.

[*Struggling to his feet.*] Usual place—same hour!

> [*He staggers to the door as* HOWARD, *in immaculate morning dress, and with a large flower in his button-hole, enters, with some sheets of paper in his hand.*

HOWARD.

Hullo, pa!

BOMPAS.

[*Pointing to* TRIMBLE.] Go with him! Help him! Scour town with him! Find her! Bring her back!

HOWARD.

Bring who—— ?

BOMPAS.

Your mother-in-law. If she meets McShane to-day [*snatching the sheets of paper from* HOWARD'S *hand*] not another bill of yours will I pay! I'll serve 'em all as I do this one! [*tearing the paper into pieces.*] You shall starve, you and your trollop of a wife! You shall sell matches in the gutter, both of you! Go—go!

> [TRIMBLE *goes out;* HOWARD *is following, but lingers doubtfully.*

MRS. BOMPAS.

Oh, Percy! Try to think all will end well. Be calm! Remember—to-night, Percy—your speech—your speech——

BOMPAS.

My speech—yes—my chance—my great chance.
[*To* HOWARD.] Well, why don't you go?

HOWARD.

Pa, ma told me to fetch the notes of your speech
from the library. You've torn 'em up.

[*He goes out.*

BOMPAS.

Ah!

[BOMPAS *and* MRS. BOMPAS *go down upon
their knees and collect the scraps of paper.*

END OF THE SECOND ACT.

THE THIRD ACT

The scene is the same as before, but it is evening.

JELF *enters, showing in* DENHAM, *who is in evening dress.*

JELF.

The ladies are dining, m'lord.

DENHAM.

Earlier than usual.

JELF.

Yes, m'lord, on account of going down to the House o' Commons.

DENHAM.

Ah, I forgot.

JELF.

The master makes a speech to-night, m'lord.

DENHAM.

I know.   Don't announce me.   I'll wait about.

[DENHAM *strolls off, then* BERYL, *in dinner dress, enters.   A piano is heard.*

BERYL.

[*To* JELF.] Who is playing the piano?

JELF.

Lord Lurgashall, miss. His lordship's just come in. [JELF *goes out.*

BERYL.

Poor Denham! I wonder how he will bear it when I let him know the decision I've come to, when I ask him plainly to release me from my engagement. I've made up my mind to do it; I'm sure it is the honest course, and I've made up my mind. It has taken me nearly a month to make it up; but, after all, a month isn't much—under—the—circumstances.
[DENHAM *returns.*

DENHAM.

Beryl! [*She gives him her hand coldly.*] You are not dining.

BERYL.

I begged to be excused half-way through dinner. My head says there's to be a thunderstorm.

DENHAM.

Ah! you are very anxious about the success of your father's speech to-night.

BERYL.

Oh, of course. He looked ghastly when he started down to the House this afternoon. By-the-by, I thought we weren't to see you till after the debate?

DENHAM.

I'm here early—on a mission.

BERYL.

A mission?

DENHAM.

I bring a message from my mother to yours.

BERYL.

Something that vexes you, by your look.

DENHAM.

I *am* vexed.

[*He is about to sit by her; she quickly places
her fan beside her on the settee.*

DENHAM.

Beryl!

BERYL.

Well?

DENHAM.

What is the matter——?

BERYL.

The matter!

DENHAM.

Between us? Almost from the very moment, a
month ago, when you and I—understood one another,
almost from that very moment you have altered
towards me! Why?

BERYL.

Why?

DENHAM.

What have I done—what do I do? If you find
faults in me, let me know them; if I disappoint you,
give me an opportunity of raising myself to the
standard you set up. Only teach me before you
punish me.

BERYL.

Denham, how you jump at conclusions!

DENHAM.

Conclusions?

BERYL.

Why accuse yourself?

DENHAM.

Whom should I —— ?

BERYL.

Isn't it barely possible that it is *I* who find it a little inconvenient to reach the standard of excellence which *you* raise?

DENHAM.

You are laughing at me!

BERYL.

Not at all. You look for a wife who is to be unconventionally sincere, don't you?

DENHAM.

Yes—and I look to you, Beryl.

BERYL.

Well, suppose on consideration, I can't promise to be more than conventionally genuine!

DENHAM.

Why, what do you mean?

BERYL.

Suppose, after all, I feel that I must drift the world's way; that I must preserve the ordinary hypocrisies, the every-day mental reservations, and hide something of my real self even from you ; that I must take my place with the sort of girl who is *fairly* honest, *moderately* candid, *pretty* good—but, oh, so unlike what you deserve, Denham !

> [*The voices of* MRS. BOMPAS, MISS CAZALET, *and* HONORIA, *are heard.*

DENHAM.

Dear Beryl, let me talk to you again this evening. Where ?

BERYL.

Go to the billiard-room, ten minutes from now.

DENHAM.

Yes, yes.

> MRS. BOMPAS, MISS CAZALET, *and* HONORIA *enter, followed by* LUCY.

MRS. BOMPAS.

[*To* DENHAM.] You here, my dear boy ! Why didn't you come to dinner ?

MISS CAZALET.

Are you going to be our cavalier down to the House, Lord Lurgashall ? Delightful !

> JELF *and another servant enter with coffee.*

BERYL.

[*To* LUCY.] Miss Tuck, you look lonely.

> [LUCY *goes to* BERYL *and sits beside her.*

MRS. BOMPAS.

[*To* DENHAM.] A message from Lady Ripstow— what is it ?

DENHAM.

May I see you alone for a moment?

MRS. BOMPAS.

Of course; before we go down to the House. We don't start yet awhile.

DENHAM.

I'm afraid you too—— ·

MRS. BOMPAS.

Yes, the thunder upsets all of us. Don't trouble about me; talk to the others.

[*Coffee is handed round.*

MRS. BOMPAS.

[*To herself.*] Oh! why don't I hear something from somebody? What is happening all this while? Oh! Oh! Oh!

[*The servants hand coffee to* MRS. BOMPAS.

MRS. BOMPAS.

Jelf.

JELF.

Yes, ma'am.

MRS. BOMPAS.

Has—Mrs. Mountrafford—come in yet?

JELF.

I b'lieve not, ma'am.

MRS. BOMPAS.

Nor Mr. Howard?

JELF.

Not yet, ma'am.

> MRS. BOMPAS.

Are you sure Mr. Trimble hasn't called or sent any message?

> JELF.

Quite sure, ma'am.

[*She drops the cream-jug with a clatter.*

> MRS. BOMPAS.

Take it away!　Don't worry me!

[*The servants go out.*

> MRS. BOMPAS.

[*To herself.*] That woman Hooley—out all day! Howard—out all day!　Not a sign from Monty! What on earth is happening?　Oh!

> MISS CAZALET.

You ought all to be very much obliged to me!　I have persuaded Miss Mountrafford to practise a few steps of the dance Cormanti is teaching her.

> MRS. BOMPAS.

Bother!

> MISS CAZALET.

[*To Mrs. Bompas.*] Isn't it good-natured of her?

> MRS. BOMPAS.

Very—so soon after dinner.

> HONORIA.

Miss Tuck, we left the music on the piano.　Will you go and thump it over for me?

[*LUCY goes out.*

MISS CAZALET.

[*Clapping her hands.*] Places! places! [*To* BERYL.]
How sweet Honoria is—and Mrs. Mountrafford!

BERYL.

They would be glad to hear you say so.

MISS CAZALET.

So unaffectedly natural. But there, think of their
strange careers! Why, this girl and her mother
might have been scalped years ago!

MRS. BOMPAS.

[*To herself.*] Oh, if they only had been!

MISS CAZALET.

Eh?

MRS. BOMPAS.

I—I didn't speak.

[*Dance music is heard.*

HONORIA.

My heart's beating!

> [HONORIA *dances gracefully, and, while
> she is dancing,* TRIMBLE *enters unobtru-
> sively, in morning dress, but dusty, dis-
> ordered, and weary-looking. He touches*
> MRS. BOMPAS *on the shoulder, and she
> utters a scream. Everybody is startled.*
> HONORIA *ceases dancing—the music stops,
> and* LUCY *appears in the doorway.*

MRS. BOMPAS.

Monty!

TRIMBLE.

I beg pardon—I alarmed you.

[HONORIA, MISS CAZALET, *and* BERYL *surround* MRS. BOMPAS.

HONORIA and MISS CAZALET.

What's the matter?

MRS. BOMPAS.

It's nothing. Don't notice me; I'm nervous to-night. Monty, I—I have something to arrange with you for Ascot week. Here!

MISS CAZALET.

Let us all go to the piano. Beryl—Lord Lurgashall.

[*They go out, and leave* TRIMBLE *and* MRS. BOMPAS *together*.

MRS. BOMPAS.

Well?

TRIMBLE.

Well?

MRS. BOMPAS.

Nothing—no news?

TRIMBLE.

No. And you? Hasn't—ah—dear Mrs. Mountrafford returned? [*She shakes her head.*] Singular—painfully singular. Where's your son? [*She shakes her head.*] H'm! It was about noon when he and I set out upon our search. I lost him at half-past four, somewhere near the Burlington Arcade. He must be very tired. *I* haven't sat down since I

started. Will you allow me ? [*As he sits.*] O-o-h !
[*Taking a lozenge.*] Dear E-B has gone down to the
House ?

MRS. BOMPAS.

Yes.

TRIMBLE.

If he had been at home I should have hesitated
about coming up. I find it difficult to excuse his
attitude of this morning.

MRS. BOMPAS.

Poor fellow !

TRIMBLE.

Thank you.

MRS. BOMPAS.

I'm thinking of Percy.

TRIMBLE.

Oh, yes. When he returns from what 1 still hope
will be an oratorical triumph, I should like you, in
justice to myself, to let him know that I have devoted
my day to his interests, loyally.

MRS. BOMPAS.

We are very much obliged to you.

TRIMBLE.

No, no. After leaving your house with dear
Howard, I found myself on the doorstep facing a
difficult problem—how to prevent a possible communication between two people who were to meet
each other at an hour and place unknown to me.
The further question as to what the deuce I should
do if I encountered them did not fail to suggest itself.

Mrs. Bompas.

Of course it was hopeless; Percy was in a frenzy.

Trimble.

Ultimately I determined that, if I succeeded in my search, I would entertain one or both of the parties with whimsical stories while Howard dashed home in a cab to fetch dear E-B. This arranged, we rapidly touched at every place of rendezvous in the West End usually selected by lovers. Here I derived the utmost assistance from Howard.

Mrs. Bompas.

There's a lot of good in that boy. But you've seen no sign of them ?

Trimble.

Not a shadow. I suppose we were too late for 'em in one place and too early in another. Oh, it has been such an unsatisfactory day ! Finally, Howard fancied he saw an Oxford man, or something, in Burlington Street and bolted away. After that I fear my search lost method. But still I never sat down. I calculate I have done Bond Street thirty-three times. I became nauseated with repeated cups of chocolate at Charbonnell's—all swallowed standing.

Mrs. Bompas.

But the result is nothing—nothing !

Trimble.

Pardon me, dear Mrs. E-B, I have proved, I hope, what friendship is capable of. And for the first time for nearly forty years I find myself at this hour *not* in evening dress.

DENHAM *enters.*

DENHAM.

1 beg pardon ; 1 thought perhaps——

TRIMBLE.

I'm off, my dear L. [*To* MRS. BOMPAS.] Good-bye, dear Mrs. E-B ; I must be at the opera to night—there's a new tenor. It's a disgrace that this big debate in the House clashes with *Otello :* lots of people are very angry about it. Love to E-B ! [*He goes out.*

MRS. BOMPAS.

[*To* DENHAM.] You want me, my dear boy ?

DENHAM.

[*Producing a letter.*] I am very sorry to have to be the bearer of this from my mother.

MRS. BOMPAS.

For me ?

DENHAM.

You have never been told, I think, that my mother has a strong aversion to Miss Cazalet.

MRS. BOMPAS.

Good gracious me, no !

DENHAM.

That refers to it.

MRS. BOMPAS.

Oh !

DENHAM.

1 wanted to see you before you read it, to say this. The letter is my mother's, not mine ; any request that

it contains is made solely by her; any threat that she holds out she will execute alone.

MRS. BOMPAS.

Threat, my dear boy!

DENHAM.

I fear you will find something of the kind there. [*He kisses her hand.*] But I beg that you will believe me, for Beryl's sake, always dutifully and affectionately yours. [*To himself.*] The billiard-room, Beryl said, in ten minutes. [*He goes out.*

MRS. BOMPAS.

[*Reading rapidly.*] "Lord Lurgashall will explain, if required, my reasons for the grave exception I take to the lady I have more than once encountered at your house. Let me say, with every amiable sentiment, that my acquaintance with you must be suspended until you undertake to close your doors upon this lady." Oh! "I need scarcely add that upon your decision now rests the question as to whether Lord Ripstow will ever call. Faithfully yours, Victoria Ripstow." Oh! Oh, in all the world is there a more unlucky woman than myself! Every hour a new trouble! And now—Lurgashall's mother! The very best person we know, too! Oh!

BOMPAS *enters, breathless and excited.*

BOMPAS.

Hullo!

MRS. BOMPAS.

Percy!

BOMPAS.

Don't be frightened. I've arranged with the Whips to be away from the House for an hour. I've come over so fidgety about Mother Hooley. Cat! Is she back?

MRS. BOMPAS.

No—nor Howard.

BOMPAS.

Oh!

MRS. BOMPAS.

Monty looked in, to say he'd had no luck.

BOMPAS.

Yah!

MRS. BOMPAS.

Percy, is—is Mr. McShane in the House?

BOMPAS.

No, not yet. I can't make out what's going on; I can't make it out. But there, I'm a fool to think of 'em. Don't mention 'em again—don't let me mention 'em! I'll think of nothing to-night but myself—myself—and my chance!

MRS. BOMPAS.

That's right.

BOMPAS.

Look here, now I'm home·I'll jump into my dress-clothes. I always speak better in dress-clothes, don't I?

MRS. BOMPAS.

Yes, yes.

BOMPAS.

I look more aristocratic in them—don't you think? Don't I look more aristocratic in my dress-clothes?

MRS. BOMPAS.

Yes.

BOMPAS.

Then why don't you encourage me? Why don't you —— ?

[*He sits down and begins quickly sorting and arranging the notes of his speech.*

BOMPAS.

My speech. One—two—three—four. Where's five—where's five?

MRS. BOMPAS.

How poorly you seem!

BOMPAS.

My brain's boiling. Eight's gone! This is a tremendous chance. Eight.

MRS. BOMPAS.

You've eaten nothing.

BOMPAS.

No. Nine.

MRS. BOMPAS.

Have a sponge cake.

BOMPAS.

Sponge——! Ugh! I tried to masticate a chop down there, but—I shall speak better on an empty stomach, sha'n't I? [*Stamping his foot violently.*] Sha'n't I speak better on an—— ?

MRS. BOMPAS.

Yes.

BOMPAS.

Then why don't you encourage me? Why don't you —— ?

MRS. BOMPAS.

Oh, Percy, I—I've got a horrible dread that—that our luck's changing!

BOMPAS.

Changing! Do you call this encouraging me? Let me go and dress!

MRS. BOMPAS.

Stay—look! [*showing him the letter.*] Here's Lady Ripstow at it now. It appears she hates Kate Cazalet.

BOMPAS.

Let her—we don't care.

MRS. BOMPAS.

But she threatens not to know me if I continue to receive Miss Cazalet here. What shall I do?

BOMPAS.

Do! *do!* Throw Kate Cazalet over, of course.

MRS. BOMPAS.

Oh, Percy!

BOMPAS.

Kindly—kindly. If the ship rides lighter without her, over with her!

MRS. BOMPAS.

How can I!

BOMPAS.

Clara, look here, I'm getting desperate! This ingratitude of Mother Hooley's is making a different man of me! Cat! Even you won't recognise me soon. I tell you, if we get well out of the scrape that we're in, I'm going to alter my line of conduct for the rest of my life.

MRS. BOMPAS.

Oh, yes, let us both do that—let us—let us!

BOMPAS.

For the future, SELF! I mean it! No more studying other people! Simply Ourselves—Ourselves! So if Lady Ripstow, or any other person of title, objects to a woman-friend of ours, over she goes—look out there!—over she goes!

MRS. BOMPAS.

Ah!

BOMPAS.

I'll go and dress. Be ready for me in a quarter-of-an-hour and I'll take you down to the House. Give me a kiss, old lady. [*She makes no response.*] Ho! this is encouragement, isn't it! Very well, I'll encourage myself. [*Snapping his fingers.*] That for Mother Hooley! Cat! That for McShane! I defy everybody! Nothing 'll ever hurt *me!* I'm a successful man! Nothing 'll ever ——! [*He goes out.*

MRS. BOMPAS.

Well, if this has to be done, I suppose I—How shall I manage it? No more lies if I can help it! Not another lie will I tell that isn't strictly necessary!

Why shouldn't I speak plainly to Kate Cazalet? As
a woman of the world she'd understand that I daren't
offend this aristocratic old reptile. That's it; I'll
throw myself on her indulgence. [*Opening the door
and calling.*] Miss Cazalet, dear!

Miss CAZALET *enters, followed by* HONORIA *and* LUCY.

MRS. BOMPAS.

[*To* MISS CAZALET.] Come upstairs — I want five
minutes of the cosiest chat with you imaginable.

MISS CAZALET.

Just what I love.

MRS. BOMPAS.

Oh, dear!

MISS CAZALET.

You're faint.

MRS. BOMPAS.

It's only the thunder. Come upstairs.

MISS CAZALET.

My dear Mrs. Bompas, let me tell you an excellent
thing for nerves——   [*They go out.*

BERYL *enters.*

BERYL.

The billiard-room in ten minutes. Poor Denham!

[*She steals off. As she does so,* HOWARD *is
heard outside the door singing a " comic
song " in a maudlin way.*

LUCY.

Hark! What's that?

HONORIA.

Why, I do believe——!

[LUCY *goes to the door and looks out.*

LUCY.

Oh! come away, Miss Mountrafford; oh, do come away.

[LUCY *drags* HONORIA *across the room, as* Howard *lurches in, drunk.*

LUCY.

Oh! Oh!

HONORIA.

Howard!

HOWARD.

I've go' back.

LUCY.

[*To* HONORIA.]   Oh, pray come upstairs!

HONORIA.

[*To* LUCY.] Ah, don't be alarmed, dear.   I've seen him—ill—once before.   [*To* HOWARD.] Are you aware of the state you're in?

HOWARD.

Am I 'ware state I'm in?   You 'lude to the fac' that I am a little dusty.

HONORIA.

Dusty, is it!   I fancy you've been laying the dust pretty well.

HOWARD.

Layin' the——?   Aha!   Good-goo'!   Layin' the dus'!   Goo'!   Is there another la'y presen', or is it all you?

HONORIA.

Sure, it's Miss Tuck.

HOWARD.

Owh! Misstuck! [*staggering towards* LUCY.] Of course—Misstuck!

LUCY.

Oh, no, please!

HOWARD.

I recklect—Misstuck—stayin' in our 'ouse—teaching Hon—Hon—nor—ror—ria. Hic!

[*He falls helplessly into a chair.*

LUCY.

Come, let us help him into his room quietly.

HONORIA.

I'll not lend a hand.

LUCY.

Oh, I know it isn't quite the way in which young women ought to occupy themselves; but suppose his people were to see him in this condition!

HONORIA.

Let them! What do I care! It'll be a lesson to 'em. They think themselves mighty superior—let 'em contemplate that! Many a lecture they've favoured me with on *my* behaviour—let 'em look at that! *I'm* not to put my knife in my mouth at mealtimes; *I'm* not to sponge up my gravy with a crust in strange houses! Let 'em look at *that!* Oh, the impudence of it!

LUCY.

I don't understand what you mean. I think you're very hard-hearted. [*Advancing to* HOWARD *and taking his arm.*] Come upstairs.

HOWARD.

[*Throwing his arms round* LUCY.] Oh, my darling! My dar—— !

LUCY.

[*Releasing herself.*] Ahh !

[HONORIA *boxes* HOWARD'S *ears and shakes him.*

HOWARD.

Wha' !

HONORIA.

I'll teach you !

HOWARD.

Wrong again !

HONORIA.

Fondling a strange lady !

HOWARD.

Strange la'y ! I thought she was you ! Oh, when do I do ri' ? I dun' know.

LUCY.

Pray overlook it, Miss Mountrafford. I'm convinced he didn' know the difference——

HONORIA.

Sure, it's time he did then !

HOWARD.

Wha' that la'y says is correc'. Oh, I have had a

dre'ful month, this las' month! Oh, my darling! my darling!

HONORIA.

[*Caressing him.*] Ah, did I strike you a blow then, dearest?

HOWARD.

Fri'ful blow.

HONORIA.

Sure, I'm unconscious of what I'm doing when my Irish blood's up. You'll forgive, Howard?

HOWARD.

Yes.

HONORIA.

And you'll never reduce yourself to this state any more?

HOWARD.

Never—hic!

HONORIA and HOWARD.

Ah!   [*They embrace lovingly.*

LUCY.

Miss Mountrafford——

HOWARD.

Go 'way! We're all ri'.

LUCY.

I must beg you to remember that you are merely engaged to Mr. Howard.

HONORIA.

Ah, mind your own business!

LUCY.

I owe a duty to those who employ me.

HONORIA.

You've only got to teach me French.

HOWARD.

[*Waving* LUCY *away.*] French!

LUCY.

And to advise you on a course of general behaviour. Miss Mountrafford, there are certain prescribed limits beyond which it is not, decorous for a young person to step during the period of engagement.

HONORIA.

Philoo!

LUCY.

I feel you are travelling beyond those limits.

[HOWARD *kisses* HONORIA.

LUCY.

Mr. Howard!

[*She advances to* HOWARD, *and drags him from the settee.*

LUCY.

I'll tell! your parents!

HOWARD.

Wha'! How dare you interfere between me— and—and my goo' lady!

HONORIA.

Howard! whist!

HOWARD.

I repea', my goo' lady.

HONORIA.

What are you saying?

HOWARD.

This is my lawful wife—my precious wife!

HONORIA.

Don't listen to him!

HOWARD.

We are on our honeymoon.

LUCY.

Miss Mountrafford——!

HOWARD.

Mountrafford! That's Mrs. Howard Egerton-Bompas——

HONORIA.

There now!

HOWARD.

Formerly Miss 'Nory-oria 'Ooley.

HONORIA.

Now he's done it!

HOWARD.

I'm sick of 'umbug and deception! I'm married gentleman! Let all the world know it! I'm young married English gentleman!

LUCY,

Oh, Mr. Howard!

HOWARD.

'Noria, I know we can trus' this sweet young lady.
Have you got your marriage certificate with you ?

[HONORIA *produces an envelope from the*
bodice of her dress.

HONORIA.

Have I got it ! Sure it never leaves me, night nor
day. [*Handing a certificate to* LUCY.] Look at that
and hold your tongue about it.

LUCY.

But this doesn't refer——

HONORIA.

Yes, yes, my dear, and we're to be married all over
again to make a fine tip-top match of it.

LUCY.

But were you never Miss Mountrafford ?

HONORIA.

Not I, sweet. [*Kissing* LUCY.] Sure, I feel easier in
my mind now that we've got one real friend in the
house.

HOWARD.

One real——! My darling !

HONORIA.

Now then !

LUCY.

Hark ! I'm sure somebody's coming.

HONORIA.

[*Supporting* HOWARD.] Hold up, dearest.
　　[LUCY *and* HONORIA *lead* HOWARD *with
　　difficulty to a door.*

HOWARD.

It's Monty Trimble's idea—'umbugging second
wedding.

HONORIA.

That's enough now—drop it!

HOWARD.

Ol' story—everybody ashamed of 'orrid ol' mother-
in-law.

HONORIA.

Come on!

HOWARD.

Ol' mother 'Ooley! ol' mother—— !
　　[*They go out, and as they disappear,* MISS
　　CAZALET *enters in a towering rage;
　　while* MRS. BOMPAS *follows, attempting
　　to pacify her.*

MISS CAZALET.

Not another word! don't speak to me!

MRS. BOMPAS.

Pray try to see things in their right light.

MISS CAZALET.

In their right light! I am taken by the shoulders
and turned out of this house——

MRS. BOMPAS.

No—no!

Miss Cazalet.

Kicked out of it—to please that woman Ripstow! That's the only light in which I see things. [*Trying to put on her mantle.*] Confound the cloak!

Mrs. Bompas.

Let me help you.

Miss Cazalet.

Hah, what a hurry you're in to see the last of me! Send Lucy to me; I'll take her away to-night. Oh, the insult, the insult!

Mrs. Bompas.

Wait here till you have spoken to my husband; he will offer every apology.

Miss Cazalet.

Apology! Let the creature Ripstow apologise. Send Lucy to me.

Mrs. Bompas.

Calm yourself! My husband is at home; I'll find him.

Miss Cazalet.

The insult! the insult!

Mrs. Bompas.

How truly unfortunate! Wait, wait! Percy, Percy!

[*She runs out.* Miss Cazalet *seizes the pillows from the settees, and the books from the table, and flings them about the room.*

MISS CAZALET.

Ah! Ah! What can I do—what can I do to
pay out this viper Ripstow! If I can't revenge myself on her I shall become frantic—frantic! Oh!

LUCY, *still clutching the marriage-certificate,
enters quickly.*

MISS CAZALET.

Lucy!

LUCY.

Oh!

MISS CAZALET.

What's wrong with you?

LUCY.

I—I'm so upset.

MISS CAZALET.

Upset!

LUCY.

I—I don't know whether I'm doing my duty here.
This seems to be such a strange household.

MISS CAZALET.

Hah, so *I* think!

LUCY.

Do you know—do you know—they are already
married?

MISS CAZALET.

Who are married?

LUCY.

Young Mr. Howard and Miss. Mountrafford. . Oh,
I oughtn't to have told you!

MISS CAZALET.

Go on !

LUCY.

You won't repeat it, will you ? And, what's more, she—she isn't Miss Mountrafford at all, and never was !

MISS CAZALET.

Lucy ! [*Snatches the certificate from* LUCY's *hand.*] What have you got there ?

LUCY.

[*Attempting to recover it.*] Oh, no ! Oh, my head !

MISS CAZALET.

[*Reading.*] " Marriage solemnised at the Register Office, in the District of St. Michael's, Abergaron, in the County of Carnarvon—Howard Bompas—Honoria Hooley !" What's the meaning of it ?

LUCY.

I—I'm dreadfully afraid it's a *mésalliance*.

MISS CAZALET.

A *mésalliance* ?

LUCY.

Yes, and poor Mr. and Mrs. Egerton-Bompas are trying to give a good aspect to the matter by cele- brating a second marriage. Oh, don't you feel sorry for them ?

MISS CAZALET.

Awfully. And this—this is the family into which the son of my old friend Lady Ripstow is about to enter ! Ha, ha, ha, ha !

Lucy.

What are you laughing at ?

Miss Cazalet.

Come home !

Lucy.

Home ?

[Miss Cazalet *crams the certificate into her pocket.*

Miss Cazalet.

You can tell me all you know about this sad affair in the cab.   Quick !

Lucy.

But I don't wish to——!

Miss Cazalet.

Come !

Lucy.

The certificate—give it me —let me return it.

Miss Cazalet.

When I've done with it.

Lucy.

No, no !

Miss Cazalet.

Now, Lady Ripstow !   [*To* Lucy.]   Come home !

[*She pulls* Lucy *to the door and they go out. Then another door is opened and* Mrs. Bompas's *voice is heard.*

Mrs. Bompas.

[*Outside.*] Percy ! Percy ! Make haste ! [*She enters the room quickly.*]   Miss Cazalet ! dear Miss Cazalet !

Bompas *enters in evening dress, which has evidently
been rather hurriedly put on.   He attempts to
make his tie into a bow as he speaks.*

BOMPAS.

Where is she?   Where is she?

MRS. BOMPAS.

She hasn't gone, surely !   Miss Cazalet !

BOMPAS.

Don't upset yourself !   Throw her over.

MRS. BOMPAS.

She must be looking for her niece.

BOMPAS.

She's of no consequence, I tell you——

MRS. BOMPAS.

[*Opening the door and calling.*] Miss Cazalet !

BOMPAS.

That rotten newspaper of hers is dead or dying ; it
can't do us either harm or good.   Over with her !

MRS. BOMPAS. .

Miss Cazalet !

[MRS. BOMPAS *goes out.*

BOMPAS.

Come and tie my bow, Clara. Clara, come and tie my bow. Clara! [*Finding she is gone.*] Oh! Miss Cazalet indeed! How my hand shakes! Over with her! I've made up my mind—for the future, Self! I—I can't tie my bow. [*Sitting helplessly at the end of the settee.*] Clara—old lady!

> [*Unnoticed by* BOMPAS, MRS. HOOLEY, *looking very much upset, and* McSHANE, *pale, speechless, and agitated, enter the room, and stand gazing at* BOMPAS.

BOMPAS.

[*To himself.*] I—I'll wait for Clara. Heavens, how does my peroration begin? [*Turning over his notes hastily.*] I—I'm forgetting my peroration.

> [MRS. BOMPAS *returns and sees* MRS. HOOLEY and McSHANE.

MRS. BOMPAS.

Percy!

BOMPAS.

Do come and tie my bow. Eh? [*Seeing* MRS. HOOLEY *and* McSHANE.] Oh!

> [McSHANE *fidgets with his umbrella.*

BOMPAS.

Mr. McShane, I—I didn't hear the servant announce you in the—the—proper way.

McSHANE.

Sir, I let myself in with this lady's latch-key.

MRS. BOMPAS.

Oh!

BOMPAS.

Oh! Er—ah—Mrs.—Mrs. Mountrafford, we rejoice to see you looking so much—better.   Don't we, Clara?

[MRS. HOOLEY *begins to sob demonstratively.*

BOMPAS.

Er—that is, I'm glad that the report of your illness, the—ah—influenza, was exaggerated.   How it got about I—I trust, Mr. McShane——   Clara?

McSHANE.

Bompas. Bompas. Cease your dirty prevarication. I know all, sir.

MRS. HOOLEY.

Owh!   And indeed it's myself that's told him the entire truth.   Oh, why was I so impulsive!

McSHANE.

Mrs. Kathleen Hooley, ma'am——

BOMPAS and MRS. BOMPAS.

[*Exchanging looks.*] Ah!

McSHANE.

Mrs. Kathleen Hooley, you'll oblige me by keeping silent—if that's possible.

MRS. HOOLEY.

Loving me as he did, I never anticipated he'd take the disclosures in this way——

McSHANE.

Mrs. Hooley——!

MRS. HOOLEY.

Sure, Kitty Hooley's as fine a woman as Kathleen Mountrafford, barring the fortune he looked for. Owh!

McSHANE.

Bompas, when I met this lady to-day at our usual place of meeting, the National Gallery·——-

BOMPAS and MRS. BOMPAS.

The National Gallery!

McSHANE.

And when I perceived that she was in more than her usual state of health, I felt I was the victim of some despicable, underhand doings of which you were the originator.

BOMPAS.

I advise you to be careful, Mr. McShane; I really advise you——

McSHANE.

But I was not prepared for the revelations of craft, cunning, and duplicity which were made over a cup of tea at a neighbouring restaurant.

BOMPAS.

Clara, note Mr. McShane's language—note it!

McSHANE.

I dashed. down to the House, to find you had skulked home for an hour; I followed you here. Now, sir! You'll be good enough to ask these ladies to retire.

K

Bompas.

Sir, I request that you communicate with me only by letter.

McShane.

You request, sir! You——!

Mrs. Hooley.

[*Clinging to him.*] Ah, Tim, Tim! We'll go, darling! Don't let your temper rise! We'll go, darling boy, we'll go!

McShane.

[*Releasing himself.*] Kathleen!

Mrs. Hooley.

Yes, yes, I'll leave you. Oh, Tim, is it all over between us?

McShane.

I—I can't say, Kathleen. It's a difficult position I'm in with regard to you. But I'll consider—there!

Mrs. Hooley.

Why was I so indiscreet! Oh, the love I've thrown away this day!

Bompas.

[*To* Mrs. Bompas.] Keep near at hand—don't leave me!

Mrs. Bompas.

I won't. We're in his power, Percy.

Bompas.

I know—I know.

Mrs. Bompas.

But be bold; brazen it out.

BOMPAS.

Yes, yes—yes, yes.

MRS. BOMPAS.

And then, if you can, buy him.

BOMPAS.

Yes, yes.

MRS. BOMPAS.

My poor old man! Shriek if you want me.

BOMPAS.

Yes, yes.

MRS. BOMPAS.

I mean, call out.

BOMPAS.

I know—same thing.

[MRS. BOMPAS *goes out with* MRS. HOOLEY.

BOMPAS.

[*To himself.*] Bold—brazen it out. Bold—brazen it out. Now, Mr. McShane, I ask the reason of this outrageous conduct—conduct unbecoming a gentleman, conduct which—— [*He sees* McSHANE *reading the notes of his speech.*] What's that you're reading—what's that you're reading?

McSHANE.

The notes of your speech, sir.

BOMPAS.

Put those down! How dare you! How dare——!

McSHANE.

What! Lift up your voice to me again and I'll

publicly proclaim you the mean, fraudulent trickster
that you undoubtedly are !

BOMPAS.

Sir !

McSHANE.

Raise your voice half a tone above your ordinary
dirty conversational level, and to-morrow all London
shall ring with the vile imposture of which you're
guilty ! '

BOMPAS.

Ah, McShane! McShane, it's you who are violent,
not—not I. I—McShane, let's talk the matter over
quietly—shall we ? Quietly—both of us—quietly—
quietly——

McSHANE.

[*Resuming his examination of the notes.*] As I
thought—as I thought.

BOMPAS.

You've no right to read those notes, McShane—no
right whatever—no—no——

McSHANE.

A contemptible vituperation of the Party to which
it is my pride to belong.

BOMPAS.

That speech, sir, is a—a—an avowal of—of the
convictions of a lifetime.

McSHANE,

See page three.

BOMPAS.

That speech contains a—a—a lucid exposition of my—my firm, undeviating political principles——

McSHANE.

Your what?

BOMPAS.

Principles which have been the main guide and factor of a busy life; principles which are—are—are——!

McSHANE.

[*Prompting him from the notes.*] Which are as vital as——

BOMPAS.

That's it—as vital as the air I breathe, as the—the——! What are you doing—what are you doing?

[McSHANE *is deliberately placing the notes in his breast-pocket. Twilight is falling.*

McSHANE.

Bompas, you will not require these notes.

BOMPAS.

What do you mean? My speech! my speech!

McSHANE.

You will not deliver this speech, Bompas.

BOMPAS.

To-night! I speak it to-night!

McSHANE.

No, sir, you do not, because from this moment you abjure the political principles which have been the main guide and factor of your busy life——

BOMPAS.

I !

McSHANE.

From this moment you turn your back on convictions which are as vital as the air you breathe——

BOMPAS.

I do not !

McSHANE.

You do ! And in their place you will adopt the views and opinions, and the mode of reasoning, of the Party to which it is my pride to belong. Bompas, you're ours !

BOMPAS.

Yours ! Yours !

McSHANE.

Yes, Bompas, from this time forth your sympathies, your aspirations, your instincts, are purely Irish. [BOMPAS *utters a low cry.*] In the House, and out of it, you're now a staunch, consistent, and, when necessary, an animated supporter of Joseph Finnerty and Michael James Shannon. Think yourself mighty lucky you're let off so pleasantly for the trick you've played me over the widow. My first, unworthy impulse was to trumpet your rascality to the world.

BOMPAS.

Oh !

McSHANE.

And then a finer, loftier inspiration came to me— to utilise you in the cause of Patriotism !

BOMPAS.

No, no!

McSHANE.

Don't imagine I'm proud of you. But the handsome and regular contributions you'll make to our Parliamentary Fund will be acceptable, and the dirtiest vote counts on a division. [*Holding out his hand.*] And so, Blankets—permanent!

BOMPAS.

Take care! You can't do this! You sha'n't do it! I defy you! I defy you!

McSHANE.

What's that!

BOMPAS.

No, no, I don't! McShane, McShane—old fellow —old chap—be open to argument! If you make a political turncoat of me, I shall lose all my big friends —nobs!—nice people who'd be glad of any excuse to give me the cold-shoulder. Don't do it, don't do it, just as I'm laying hold of their coat-tails!

McSHANE.

Ah, I'm ashamed of you!

BOMPAS.

McShane—dear old boy! I *will* support your Parliamentary Fund, munificently,—I will, I will; only let me do it in a quiet, unostentatious, anonymous way, and don't stop me from abusing your Party in the House! McShane, McShane!

McSHANE.

What! You're asking me to be a schemer and a

hypocrite like yourself, are you! No, sir! I'm an
injured man—my feelings are outraged, my affections
misplaced ; but it's a convert I'm making, not a
victim. It's no use, Bompas—you're ours.

BOMPAS.

Clara! [*To* McSHANE.] You'd strangle my parliamentary career! Clara! You'd put your heel on the
neck of a rising politician! Clara! Clara! Clara!
[MRS. BOMPAS *enters.*] Clara!

MRS. BOMPAS.

I know—I've been listening.

BOMPAS.

My chance! my chance!

MRS. BOMPAS.

Mr. McShane! The great opportunity of my poor
husband's life!

McSHANE.

Don't distress yourself, ma'am. We'll give him
magnificent opportunities by-and-by,—long nights
of 'em.

MRS. BOMPAS.

But this night! Man, haven't you any heart!
We're all ready to go down!

McSHANE.

I'm extremely sorry, but in view of his abrupt
change of political views it would be better for him
not to go back to the House this evening.

Mrs. Bompas.

Oh !

Bompas.

I will go down!   I will !

McShane.

If you do, mind, you'll follow us boys into the
lobby.

Bompas.

Ahh !

McShane.

[*To* Mrs. Bompas.] Now, d'ye notice how agitated
he is ?   Let him have a quiet evening at home.

Mrs. Bompas and Bompas.

At home !   [Bompas *sinks into a chair, dazed.*

Mrs. Bompas.

Never mind, Percy.   You—used to be—fond—of
your home.

McShane.

To-morrow morning I'll look in early and dictate a
manifesto to his constituents.   And now I'll hurry
down and give the boys the intelligence.

Mrs. Bompas.

Mr. McShane !   Mr. McShane !

McShane.

Be easy, ma'am—on behalf of Joseph Finnerty
and Michael James Shannon, I promise you this.
You're ambitious, I believe, you and Blankets—
Bompas ?

Mrs. Bompas.

I don't know—perhaps—yes.

McShane.

Mrs. Bompas, in the future, *your* house shall be the centre of a great political world; *your* establishment the axis of a mighty movement; *your* drawing-room a crowded *salon*—the meeting-place of a powerful, irresistible Party.

Mrs. Bompas.

Party?

McShane.

The Party to which it is now your husband's pride to belong. [*He goes out. It is now dusk.*

Bompas.

[*Folding his arms and glaring wildly around him.*] "Mr. Speaker—sir. Nothing but a stern sense of public duty; nothing but an acute perception of the obligation I am under to my constituents—— "

Mrs. Bompas.

Percy! hush!

Bompas.

"Nothing less would have induced me to follow the torrent of eloquence which has just preceded me with the feeble trickle of my own earnest but inadequate oratory. Conscious—— "

Mrs. Bompas.

No, no!

BOMPAS.

" Hah, these interruptions do not find me unprepared ! I am not unnerved by the howling of Irish wolves——— ! "

MRS. BOMPAS.

For mercy's sake, be quiet !

BOMPAS.

" Sir, if that expression is not in accord with the courtesies practised in this House——— "

MRS. BOMPAS.

What are you thinking about ?   Old man !

BOMPAS.

" If——— "   Oh ?   Eh ?   Clara !

MRS. BOMPAS.

Yes, yes, it's Clara—Clara.

BOMPAS.

Oh, my speech, my speech !

JELF *appears.*

MRS. BOMPAS.

What is it ?

JELF.

The carriage is at the door, ma'am.

MRS. BOMPAS.

[*To* BOMPAS.] Shall I—tell him ?   [*With an effort* BOMPAS *nods assent.*] Your master does not go down to the House to-night.

JELF.

Not, ma'am !

Mrs. Bompas.

No. Send the carriage back to the stables. Turn up the light !

[Jelf *disappears quickly. The room is brightly illuminated by electric light.*

Mrs. Bompas.

Come, Percy ! Be a man ! We're not crushed yet.

Bompas.

Not crushed yet.

Mrs. Bompas.

After all, we've only changed our political views from—purely—conscientious motives. Heaven forgive us !

Bompas.

Yes, yes—conscientious motives; that's it—yes, yes.

Mrs. Bompas.

Besides, think, our danger's over. We've bought that little wretch's silence. We're safe—our danger's passed—we're safe !

Bompas.

Safe ! Yes, of course we are—safe !

Mrs. Bompas.

Nothing stops us now !

Bompas.

Nothing ! Nothing !

Mrs. Bompas

Beryl will be married next month—gloriously

married. Our Beryl, Lady Lurgashall! Think of it! think of it!

BOMPAS.

Lady Lurgashall! The future Countess of Rip-stow! Our Beryl!

MRS. BOMPAS.

Ha, ha, ha! Old man! Eh?

BOMPAS.

Ha, ha! ha, ha!

BOTH.

Ha, ha! ha, ha!

[*They link arms, laughing and chuckling.*

BERYL *enters.*

BERYL.

Mamma.

MRS. BOMPAS.

We—were—just talking about you, child.

BERYL.

Mamma, I don't know how I am to tell you.

MRS. BOMPAS.

Tell me—what?

BERYL.

Lord Lurgashall has just left the house.

MRS. BOMPAS.

Why, of course, he was to meet us at——

BERYL.

No, no, you don't see what I mean. He has left this house for ever; he will never return.

Mrs. Bompas and Bompas.

What !

BERYL.

I have told him that I cannot marry him, and our engagement is at an end.

[Bompas *advances excitedly to* Beryl; Mrs. Bompas *clings to his arm.*

Mrs. Bompas.

No, no, Percy ! This shall be put right to-morrow —a lover's quarrel.

BERYL.

It is nothing of the kind. My mind is made up. I will help to deceive our set about Howard's marriage, —you can make me do that; but you shall not make me deceive the poor fellow who wishes to marry me because of my honesty.

BOMPAS.

Ahhh !

Mrs. Bompas.

Beryl.

BERYL.

Understand me ! You sha'n't shake me ! I mean it—I mean it !   [*She goes out.*

Mrs. Bompas.

Our—children ! Our——

Bompas.

Our—children ! Ho, yes !

Mrs. Bompas.

No, no, not our children—not both of them.

There's still Howard,   Poor boy, he's been imprudent, but [*sobbing*] he's a nice boy at heart.

HOWARD *staggers on, in evening dress, his hat on the back of his head, a large flower in his button-hole, a cigar in his mouth.*

HOWARD.

Tha's ri', 'On-or-ror-ria, you practise your scales while I'm gone. You—— Ullo, ma, you 'ere! I'm off out for th' evenin'.

MRS. BOMPAS.

Howard!

HOWARD.

Wha's ma'rrer? 'Ullo, pa! Th' servants say you're not goin' down to 'Ouse of Com's to-night after all. Funked-it, hey—funked it!   Hic!

MRS. BOMPAS and BOMPAS.

Oh!

HOWARD.

So I've told 'On—or—ror—ria to pound away at her scales for an hour or so while I 'ave look round. Bye-bye!

MRS. BOMPAS.

[*Seizing him by the lapels of his coat.*] Wretch!

BOMPAS.

[*Taking him by the coat-collar.*] Blackguard!

HOWARD.

At me again!   When do I do ri'?   I dun' know.

BOMPAS.

You—you're not sober!

HOWARD.

No, I am *not* sober! I've 'ad dre'ful month, this las' month, and I am drowning my misfortunes in the bowl. Le' me alone! [*Snapping his fingers in* BOMPAS'S *face.*] There! I'm my own master! I'm young married English gentleman—with Uni—university education!

> [*He goes out,* MRS. BOMPAS *and* BOMPAS *sit staring blankly before them.* HONORIA *is heard practising her* "*scales*" *in another room.* MRS. BOMPAS *creeps over to her husband and puts her arms round him.*

END OF THE THIRD ACT.

THE FOURTH ACT

The scene is the same as before, but it is now early morning of the day subsequent to the events of the previous act.

BOMPAS, *still in evening dress, but looking very much crumpled, is asleep on the settee.* JELF *enters, whistling.*

JELF.

The gov'nor! Why, he hasn't been to bed all night! Phew!

> [*He is walking away on tiptoe, when he meets* MRS. BOMPAS *entering the room, dressed in a morning wrapper, and looking pale and agitated.*

MRS. BOMPAS.

Jelf, I am anxious about your master; he is not in his room. I can't think——

JELF.

All right, ma'am. There he is; he must have dropped off here.

MRS. BOMPAS.

Oh! [JELF *goes out.*

Mrs. Bompas.

What can he have been doing all the night long?
[*Turning over a litter of papers on the table.*] "To the
Electors of the Northern Division of St. Swithin's."
[Bompas *moans.*] Poor old man! [*Reading.*] "Gentle-
men. Actuated solely by conscientious motives——"
[Bompas *mutters in his sleep.*] He's dreaming,—
hark!

Bompas.

[*In his sleep.*] "Mr. Speaker—sir!"

Mrs. Bompas.

Oh, dear!

Bompas.

"Nothing but a stern sense of public duty——"

Mrs. Bompas.

That miserable speech!

Bompas.

"Nothing but an acute perception——"

Mrs. Bompas.

Stop! [*Shaking him.*] Percy!

Bompas.

[*Opening his eyes.*] Eh?

Mrs. Bompas.

Wake, wake! [*He starts to his feet.*] Where are you
going?

BOMPAS.

The Division—the Division !

MRS. BOMPAS.

No, no—you're at home. It's morning.

BOMPAS.

At home—morning—I've been dozing—I——[*Sees his notes on the table.*] "Gentlemen. Actuated solely by conscientious motives——" I—I remember.
> [*He looks broken down, and much older than in the previous acts.*

MRS. BOMPAS.

What have you been doing all night ?

BOMPAS.

Trying to furnish my constituents with my reasons for becoming a member of the Irish Party.

MRS. BOMPAS.

Can't you—manage it ?

BOMPAS.

No. I began in the library, but my ideas wouldn't flow. I've started afresh in nearly every room in the house, but my ideas won't flow. I don't get any further than "conscientious motives."

MRS. BOMPAS.

Old man, do you remember twenty years ago when you'd just sold our business at Kennington, and bought the two shops which were to grow into our present colossal establishment ?

BOMPAS.

Rather, as if it were yesterday.

MRS. BOMPAS.

And do you remember how we sat down together, you and I, and drew up an announcement to our old customers?

BOMPAS.

Yes.

MRS. BOMPAS.

" Percy Bompas has the honour to hope——"

BOMPAS.

" That in embarking upon his great enterprise in the West End of London——"

MRS. BOMPAS.

" He will not lose the support and good-will of those old friends——"

BOMPAS.

" Who have laid the foundation of his present prosperity." Ah!

MRS. BOMPAS.

Our ideas used to flow in those days, old man, didn't they?

BOMPAS.

I—I suppose it was because we were younger.

MRS. BOMPAS and BOMPAS.

[*Sighing.*] Ahh!   [*He sits beside her.*

BOMPAS.

That was when we took a house at Haverstock Hill; do you remember?

MRS. BOMPAS.

Do I remember! Our first home this side of the water.

BOMPAS.

[*Sadly.*] How we have got on since then!

MRS. BOMPAS.

Haven't we? It was a nice house though.

BOMPAS.

You think so because we did so much to it ourselves.

MRS. BOMPAS.

I put up the short blinds in the bedrooms with my own hands—I know that. I preferred doing it.

BOMPAS.

I hung every blessed picture in that house. I can almost feel the blisters from the cord now.

MRS. BOMPAS.

I wonder what we should think of it all to-day if we could see it again.

BOMPAS.

Not much—after this.

MRS. BOMPAS.

I suppose not; we've got on so since then, haven't we?

BOMPAS.

Rather.

MRS. BOMPAS and BOMPAS.

[*Sighing.*] Ahh! [*She gently puts her hand in his.*

Mrs. Bompas.

Our first big half-past-seven dinner-party; do you remember?

Bompas.

Oh, lor' yes, Clara—never mind that.

Mrs. Bompas.

Well, dear, we were inexperienced then. We gave them plenty to eat though, eh?

Bompas.

It took you half an hour to write each *menu.*

Mrs. Bompas.

Part of the food was sent in, I recollect, and part of it was done at home.

Bompas.

It doesn't matter much now—many that were there won't clatter another knife and fork—but to this day I regret the part of it that was done at home.

Mrs. Bompas.

My face burns too, after all these years, when I think of it.

Bompas.

Do you remember where cook's cap was found?

Mrs. Bompas.

Be quiet!

Bompas.

That was the night, too, when we had one of our men from the shop, with "P. Bompas" round his coat-collar, to announce the guests.

MRS. BOMPAS.

It seemed all right then.

BOMPAS.

Yes, by Jove, it's astonishing how we've got on since.

MRS. BOMPAS and BOMPAS.

Ahh !

BOMPAS.

Well, I suppose I'd better change my clothes.

MRS. BOMPAS.

Percy. Percy, old man, do you ever feel you'd like to go back ?

BOMPAS.

Back ?

MRS. BOMPAS.

I mean, to keep our experience, but to go back to the contented, simple part of the old times.

BOMPAS.

It's no good wishing that, Clara. When you've got knowledge you've lost everything else. It seems to me there's only one thing to do in this world—to go on; even if you're on the wrong road, Clara, my dear, get on, get on.

TRIMBLE *enters, clutching a newspaper and much agitated.*

TRIMBLE.

Here you are ! Oh, dear friends !

BOMPAS.

Trimble !

MRS. BOMPAS.

Monty!

TRIMBLE.

Have you seen it?

MRS. BOMPAS.

Seen what?

TRIMBLE.

The Morning Message.

MRS. BOMPAS.

Miss Cazalet's paper!

BOMPAS.

Ah! Anything about me?

TRIMBLE.

Anything about *you!* Say *us, us,* dear E-B! It's all out!

MRS. BOMPAS.

Out!

BOMPAS.

What's all out?

TRIMBLE.

The whole bag o' tricks. And she has had the temerity to drag me into it—me, *me!* Look, look— in the "Everybody's Friend" column! [*Reading.*] "A Fraud on Society."

MRS. BOMPAS.

Great powers!

TRIMBLE.

"It is time that some light should be thrown on the projected marriage of the son of a wealthy Member of Parliament and the daughter of a mysterious Hibernian widow, who is stated to have passed some years of her life in improving the condition of the Dakota Indians."

MRS. BOMPAS and BOMPAS.

Mrs. Mountrafford!

TRIMBLE.

Wait! " As a matter of fact, the accepted history of the widow's antecedents is a pure invention."

MRS. BOMPAS.

You're so slow! [*She snatches the paper from him.*

MRS. BOMPAS.

[*Reading.*] " A marriage has already taken place between the parties before the Registrar of a remote district in Wales, and the second ceremony is a barefaced attempt to palm off on Society the young woman and her mother, under assumed names, as people of some distinction."

[*The paper drops from* MRS. BOMPAS'S *hand.*

TRIMBLE.

Good gracious me, you're missing the most outrageous part of it, dear Mrs. E-B! This is the allusion which will rouse your indignation. Listen. [*Reading.*] " We believe we are correct in stating that the audacious conspiracy owes its inception to an honourable dear friend of the young husband's family." There! Can there be any question as to whom that points? I've never been so upset. My position in Society is at stake. What am I to do? Dear friends! Really!

Not a word of sympathy! Upon my soul, this is— I regret to employ the term—very like ingratitude.

MRS. BOMPAS.

[*To herself.*] After all—after everything—held up to the whole world!

TRIMBLE.

Naturally, the first step you will take is to deny these assertions indignantly.

MRS. BOMPAS.

Deny! They can be proved to the hilt.

TRIMBLE.

Well, well, but at the worst you can declare that you have yourselves been cruelly deceived.

MRS. BOMPAS.

No, no, I—I can't.

TRIMBLE.

You can't! Dear—dear friends, I—I admit that I am for once slightly swayed by personal considerations. Pray remember what you owe to *me!*

MRS. BOMPAS.

Who has betrayed us?

TRIMBLE.

Obviously, McShane. That detestable widow must have told him, and he——

MRS. BOMPAS.

No, no—we've secured his silence.

TRIMBLE.

You have !

BOMPAS.

Mr. Trimble, you are not aware that I am a member of the Irish Party.

TRIMBLE.

No !

BOMPAS.

Yes—yes.

TRIMBLE.

And after the way I've laboured for you in the very highest Conservative circles ! Then the traitor must be here, in your own establishment, dear Mrs. E-B. You must put your finger upon him or her before we go further. Pray, let us summon every interested person.

[MRS. BOMPAS *and* TRIMBLE *pull the bell-ropes.*

MRS. BOMPAS.

What's the use of it ?

TRIMBLE.

The use of it ! Dear lady, do try to consider the terrible position in which my good-nature has placed me !

JELF *enters.*

JELF.

[*To* BOMPAS—*in a low voice.*] I don't know whether you'll see anybody, sir, but——

TRIMBLE.

Jelf, your mistress desires to speak to Mrs. Mountrafford, Miss Mountrafford, Mr. Howard, and Miss Beryl, here, at once.

JELF.

Yes, sir, but——

TRIMBLE.

Do you hear? At once! Really!

[JELF *withdraws.*

TRIMBLE.

Ouf! There are certain contingencies which I believe even the keenest intellect—— Good gracious!

MRS. BOMPAS.

What?

TRIMBLE.

Why, look, look! What's the meaning of this?

MISS CAZALET *enters, pale, agitated, and in tears.*

TRIMBLE, MRS. BOMPAS, and BOMPAS.

Miss Cazalet!

MISS CAZALET.

You—you know what I've done?

MRS. BOMPAS.

Oh, you wicked woman! How can you show your face here!

MISS CAZALET.

You do know. Oh, I am so wretched!

MRS. BOMPAS.

Wretched !

MISS CAZALET.

Listen, dear—I don't mean dear, I mean Mrs.
Bompas. I was quite mad last night ; mad with
vexation, indignation, anything you like to call it.
Just think ! To be kicked out of a decent house by
an old woman you hate ! Ah, even now, when I'm
sorry, I could slap her in the face !

MRS. BOMPAS.

What have you come here to say—not this ?

TRIMBLE.

Sssh ! sssh ! sssh !

MISS CAZALET.

When I left here I had only one idea in my head,
to be revenged on her. Oh, if I could have got hold
of her husband, as I might have done years ago,
what a fool I would have made of him !

MRS. BOMPAS.

Miss Cazalet !

MISS CAZALET.

Well, I rushed down to Boswell Court—you know,
the office of the *M. M.*—in a fury. I saw that by
discrediting your family I could humiliate the
woman whose son is engaged to your daughter, and
I scribbled those lines. Ah, I almost wrote them with
my nails !

MRS. BOMPAS.

Cruel ! heartless !

Miss Cazalet.

Then I supped at the club, off biscuits and champagne, and went home to bed. To bed! Look at the rings round my eyes! I declare I haven't slept a wink. Look here, I'm downright sorry—there! You've been very kind to me, you and your stupid husband—I beg your pardon, there he is; and I've behaved like a—what you please—to sacrifice you to hit Lady Ripstow. So now, tell me what to do to put things right; I'll do anything while I'm in a penitent mood like this—anything. Oh, I'm an inconsistent, miserable, ill-conditioned woman, and have been all my life!

Trimble.

[*To* Mrs. Bompas.] Most fortunate. An ample apology to myself and others in her paper to-morrow will set things straight.

Mrs. Bompas.

Never; some busybody is sure to inquire further and discover the facts.

Trimble.

Of course, of course. We must divert the suspicion from ourselves. I have it! She must publicly and explicitly apologise to some other family. It's all right—I remember a similar case in which I—— [*Taking a lozenge.*] Now, what you have to do, dear Miss Cazalet, is to place yourself unreservedly in my hands——

Miss Cazalet.

Your hands! What business is it of yours?

TRIMBLE.

Dear lady, you forget I am the person most grossly libelled !

MISS CAZALET.

Oh, of course, I've mentioned you, haven't I ?

TRIMBLE.

Mentioned me !

MRS. BOMPAS.

[*Looking through the doorway.*] Mrs. Mountrafford !

TRIMBLE.

[*To* MISS CAZALET.] Come into the next room and I'll advise you in your terrible difficulty.   Come, come.

MISS CAZALET.

Mr. Bompas—Mr. Bompas—when I go down to the office I'll instruct some one to write a short complimentary leader on your last night's speech. [BOMPAS *raises his head. She is startled at his appearance.*] Ah !

BOMPAS.

Madam, I never spoke.

TRIMBLE.

Sssh, sssh !   He's a member of the Irish Party. Come along.

> [*As* TRIMBLE *and* MISS CAZALET *go out,*
> MRS. HOOLEY *enters, followed by* HONO-
> RIA *and* BERYL.

MRS. HOOLEY.

You've heard from him !

MRS. BOMPAS.

Him!

BOMPAS.

Tim! He's repented of his unkindness! He's—— !

MRS. BOMPAS.

[*Handing her the newspaper.*] Look at this, all of you! Read it! read it!

[MRS. HOOLEY, HONORIA, *and* BERYL *read the newspaper.*

MRS. BOMPAS.

Now see what you and your daughter have brought us to!

MRS. HOOLEY.

Owh!

HONORIA.

Oh, mother!

MRS. HOOLEY.

Oh, the unfavourable comments!

MRS. BOMPAS.

Who is it that has helped to bring this final disgrace upon us—that is what we want to know. Dishonourable as we've been, Mr. Bompas and I haven't quite deserved this. There, my heart's broken!

BERYL.

Mamma!

MRS. BOMPAS.

Go away! You've been against us all through. Your sympathy's no good; Pa and I don't want it.

MRS. HOOLEY.

Oh, the uncomplimentary allusions!

> [BERYL *steals over to* BOMPAS *and sits beside him.*

BOMPAS.

Berry!

BERYL.

Papa dear.

BOMPAS.

Ah! you can crow over ma and me now. This is your triumph, this is.

BERYL.

My triumph! [*slipping her arm through his and laying her head upon his shoulder.*] Oh, papa, just think!

LADY RIPSTOW *and* DENHAM *enter.*

MRS. BOMPAS.

Lady Ripstow! Lord Lurgashall!

BERYL.

[*To herself.*] Denham!   [*She goes out quickly.*

MRS. BOMPAS.

Percy! Percy!

> [BOMPAS *raises his head with an effort, then lets it sink again.*

LADY RIPSTOW.

I am painfully distressed. You have seen that terrible woman's newspaper? [Mrs. BOMPAS *nods.*] To my horror 1 find that one of the maids has allowed the wretched news-sheet to be brought into my house, and so these paragraphs have come under my notice. Of course you give an emphatic denial to the hideous charges. '

MRS. BOMPAS.

[*Trying ineffectually to rouse* BOMPAS.] Percy! Oh!

LADY RIPSTOW.

Surely—Lurgashall! Ah, here are the two ladies who are implicated! Mrs. Mountrafford, Miss Mountrafford, I ask for your assurance that there is not the slightest foundation for these abominable insinuations.

MRS. HOOLEY.

Oh, the misfortunes that have come on us!

HONORIA.

Mother, darling!

[MRS. HOOLEY *and* HONORIA *sit, embracing and weeping.*

LADY RIPSTOW.

I—I understand. [*To* DENHAM.] Take me away!

MRS. BOMPAS.

Lady Ripstow, you evidently don't know—Lord Lurgashall has not told you——

LADY RIPSTOW.

What?

MRS. BOMPAS.

His engagement to Beryl is broken off.

LADY RIPSTOW.

[*Turning to* DENHAM.] Broken off?

DENHAM.

Last night.

LADY RIPSTOW.

My son—my boy! The relief is too great! I—I can hardly credit it! And to think—that—up to yesterday—there was some question of—Lord Ripstow—calling! [*She sinks into a chair.*

DENHAM.

[*To* MRS. BOMPAS.] Don't be alarmed. My mother is always like this at the end of the Season. I think her drops are in the carriage. [*He goes out.*

LUCY TUCK, *pale, red-eyed, and trembling, enters quietly.*

HONORIA.

Miss Tuck!

LUCY.

Mrs. Bompas!

MRS. BOMPAS.

Child!

LUCY.

Oh, Mrs. Bompas, they think I've come back for my boxes—but please, please hear what I've got to say. I have seen the paper—this dreadful thing in the paper! It's my fault that it's there—all my fault.

MRS. BOMPAS.

Your fault?

LUCY.

Yes, when your son told me the secret of his marriage——

MRS. BOMPAS.

My boy told you ?   Howard !

BOMPAS.

Ah !

HOWARD *enters, wearing a gaily-coloured
morning-jacket.*

HOWARD.

Do you want me, pa ?

BOMPAS.

Do I—I—I—— !

MRS. BOMPAS.

Percy !   No, no !

HOWARD.

Here ! what now ?   At me again !

BOMPAS.

I—I—I—— !

MRS. BOMPAS.

Oh dear, oh dear !

[BOMPAS *sinks back on to the settee.*
HONORIA *seizes* HOWARD *and drags him
away.*

HONORIA.

Come away, now !

HOWARD.

When do I do right !   I dun'——

[*The newspaper is put into his hands.*

LUCY.

Oh, don't blame him—blame me! For instead of keeping the secret as I ought to have done, I blurted it out to my—my—my aunt, and now—now! Oh, you will forgive her!

MRS. BOMPAS.

Forgive her!

LUCY.

Yes, yes, you must. A friend has just called in at our lodgings to say that unless every syllable of what aunt has stated can be substantiated, she could be sent to prison for a vindictive libel! To prison!

LADY RIPSTOW.

Certainly!

LUCY.

Lady Ripstow! I didn't——

LADY RIPSTOW.

And if ever a woman deserved such a fate——!

LUCY.

Ah, no, but you wouldn't do it, would you! You wouldn't do it! Mr. Bompas—Mrs. Bompas—oh, please, please! You don't know—you don't know——!

MISS CAZALET enters, followed by TRIMBLE.

MISS CAZALET.

Lucy!

LUCY.

[*Throwing her arms impulsively around* MISS CAZALET.] Oh, mother, mother!

MRS. BOMPAS.

Mother?

LADY RIPSTOW.

Mother?

MISS CAZALET.

Lady Ripstow! [*Whispering to* LUCY, *disengaging herself.*] You little——! I—I knew you'd do this some day!

LUCY.

[*Whispering to* MISS CAZALET.] I didn't mean to—! It escaped me!

MISS CAZALET.

[*To* LUCY.] Hush! Run away, child. I'll follow you. [LUCY *goes out with faltering steps.*] Sweet girl! How fond we are of each other! [*To* MRS. BOMPAS.] I am teaching her to call me Mother. You heard her? It is only affection's little comedy, but the mere name soothes a lonely woman.

LADY RIPSTOW.

Ahh!

MISS CAZALET.

[*To* MRS. BOMPAS, *offering her hand.*] Good-bye.

[MRS. BOMPAS, *half-frightened, shakes hands with her.*

MRS. BOMPAS.

G—good—bye.

Miss Cazalet.

Lady Ripstow, you're looking very old. When Lord Ripstow once did me the honour of calling upon me he told me that he was a great admirer of *young* women. Think that over. Good-day. [*She goes out.*

Lady Ripstow.

It isn't true. Fiend ! It isn't true.

Mrs. Bompas.

Lady Ripstow !

Trimble.

Dear Lady R. !

Lady Ripstow.

Lurgashall ! Where is Lurgashall ?

Jelf *shows in* McShane, *who carries a newspaper. Directly* Mrs. Hooley *sees* McShane *she hovers about him persistently.*

McShane.

I see him. [*Showing newspaper.*] Mr. Bompas, I'll trouble you to look at that. Ah, I see you've seen it. Upon my soul, sir, I'm disheartened. Is this the way you keep a delicate family secret ? To think that such an exposure should occur on the very morning the leading papers chronicle your conversion to the Irish party !

Mrs. Hooley.

Tim.

McShane.

What's that ?

Mrs. Hooley.

Tim, darling.

McShane.

Good morning, ma'am; I'm talking to Mr. Bompas on political matters. [*To* Bompas.] Oh, it makes me sick to contemplate it! Badly as we wanted you, we can't take you with a disgraceful accusation hanging over you. People are so fastidious nowadays. Go away, Kathleen. [*Returning to* Bompas.] But understand me now, we sha'n't part with you without a struggle. [*To* Mrs. Hooley.] I'm speaking privately, ma'am. [*To* Bompas.] Somehow or other we must bottle the horrible affair up—the Party will help. If we don't succeed, sir, I warn you, we'll not have you with us; we will not be polluted by you! We'll not —— Will you leave us, Kitty? Oh, the vexation this'll be to Michael James Shannon! Look here, ma'am, now—Oh, the disgust of Jo Finnerty!

Trimble.

Dear Mr. McS.!

McShane.

Your confidential adviser. [*To* Mrs. Hooley.] If you don't release my coat, ma'am——

Trimble.

Now I know you've seen the monstrous paragraphs which have appeared this morning.

McShane.

Seen——!

Trimble.

I thought so. But, dear Mr. McShane, I hope you don't need my assurance that those very personal allusions are not intended to refer to our dear friend there at all——

McSHANE.

Not intended——!

TRIMBLE.

And, what is more, the next, and I believe final, issue of that unhappy journal will tender the humblest apology to the actual family so mercilessly libelled; some very worthy people of the name of Higginson, I am informed.

McSHANE.

[*To* TRIMBLE.] I grasp the move, Mr. Trimble; I understand, sir. [*To* BOMPAS.] Well, well, then I suppose you'll be permitted to make your first contribution to our Parliamentary Fund in the course of to-morrow. Ah, but I'm ashamed of both of you! Oh, the trickery of it! Oh, the——! What is it, Kitty? [*He retires with* MRS. HOOLEY.

MRS. BOMPAS.

Percy——

LADY RIPSTOW.

What I have to say, Mr. Bompas, is that, under the circumstances, I deem it my duty not to altogether withdraw my friendship from your family.

TRIMBLE.

Charming!

LADY RIPSTOW.

My old friend, Mr. Trimble, has hurriedly explained to me the weak but amiable way in which he allowed himself to be dragged into this affair——

TRIMBLE.

I don't regret it.

LADY RIPSTOW.

And I gather that means have been taken to avert disgrace. During the brief remainder of the present Season, therefore, we shall exchange greetings upon meeting as usual.

TRIMBLE.

This is quite delightful. And so things in this really charming house will go on in the same old pleasant routine, just as before.

MRS. BOMPAS.

Just as before.

BOMPAS.

Just as before.

LADY RIPSTOW.

With the exception, of course——

TRIMBLE.

Oh, dear Lurgashall and—ahem! Of course. Otherwise, just as before.

MRS. BOMPAS and BOMPAS.

[*To themselves.*] Just as before.

TRIMBLE.

Just—as—before.

BOMPAS.

No! No! No!

[*There is a general movement of surprise.*

DENHAM *and* BERYL *enter*.

MRS. BOMPAS.

Percy!

TRIMBLE.

Dear E-B !

BOMPAS.

[*To* MRS. BOMPAS.] Sit down !

MRS. BOMPAS.

Why—— ?

BOMPAS.

Sit down, old lady. Take a sheet of paper—quick, Clara !—and write—write—write !

MRS. BOMPAS.

What—what ?

BOMPAS.

[*Dictating.*] " To the Editor of *The Times.* Sir."

[MRS. BOMPAS *writes*.

McSHANE.

What ails him ? [*Gripping* LADY RIPSTOW's *arm*.] Kathleen—I beg your pardon. [*Turning to* MRS. HOOLEY.] Kathleen !

BOMPAS.

[*Dictating.*] " Permit me to announce to my constituents, through your columns, that I intend to immediately resign my seat in the House——

MRS. BOMPAS.

[*Writing.*] Percy !

TRIMBLE.

Dear friend !

McSHANE.

Mr. Bompas, are you demented ?

BOMPAS.

[*To* McSHANE.] Keep away from me ! Keep away !

McSHANE.

[*Retreating against* LADY RIPSTOW.] Kathleen ! I beg your pardon. [*To* MRS. HOOLEY.] Kathleen !

BOMPAS.

[*Dictating.*] " ——to retire from business, and to reside abroad."

TRIMBLE.

Now, dear E-B, I must speak a word—— !

HOWARD.

Oh ! Here, pa—— !

McSHANE.

Upon my soul—— ! [*To* LADY RIPSTOW.] Excuse me.

BOMPAS.

[*Dictating.*] " Your obedient servant."

TRIMBLE, McSHANE and HOWARD.

No, no, no !

BOMPAS.

Ring the bell, Clara—ring the bell ! [MRS. BOMPAS *rings.*] [*Writing.*] " Percy — Bompas." No Egerton. Damn the Egerton !

LADY RIPSTOW and MRS. HOOLEY.

Oh !

McShane.

Oh, the vile language!

[Bompas *addresses and seals the letter.*

Trimble.

But—but—but, dear E-B, you're undoing all I've done for you! This is practically an admission of—of everything that's unpleasant!

McShane.

Absolutely!

Lady Ripstow.

Without doubt!

Mrs. Hooley.

Ah, he's ruining my character for me!

Jelf *enters.*

Bompas.

[*To* Jelf.] By messenger.

Trimble.

Dear friend, pause—pause! You are fatally compromising *me!*

Bompas.

Tout! meddler! go-between!

Trimble.

My position in Society! I—I——!

Bompas.

[*Handing the letter to* Jelf.] By messenger—at once! [Jelf *withdraws.*

Trimble.

A confession—and I involved! A confession!

BOMPAS.

Yes, a confession. Clara—old lady—I—I've broken down. My head's gone—I can't stand it any longer. Take me away—out of it—out of it!

MRS. BOMPAS.

Yes, yes, Percy.

BOMPAS.

I wasn't always as I am now. It is "getting on in the world" that has ruined me. I've thought of it all-night through. A self-taught man must always be a proud fool; he has a double share of vanity— the vanity of the ready pupil and the vanity of the successful tutor combined! He is blown out till he bursts! I say there ought to be a law to stop men like me from "getting on" beyond a certain point. Prosperity weakens our brains and hardens our hearts; it takes honest friends from us and seats things like that [*pointing to* TRIMBLE] in their chairs; it spoils good wives and breeds bad children——!

MRS. BOMPAS.

No, no, Percy—it hasn't utterly spoilt me. I'm tired too. We'll go away together, you and I, old man, to some place where we're not known, and we'll try back—shall we, shall we? [*She kneels beside him.*] All right, Percy—cheer up, old man!

HOWARD.

Here, ma! This is a nice blow to my prospects in life!

HONORIA.

Come away! You've got me.

McSHANE.

[*To himself.*] Well, well, I suppose I'll explain matters to Michael James Shannon and Mr. Finnerty as best I can. I've done my utmost for the Party, and if Mr. Finnerty gives me any of his temper— but I'll not anticipate. [*Contemplating* BOMPAS.] Upon my soul, that's a humiliating spectacle! Oh, the moral I could draw from it. [MRS. BOMPAS *looks round at him fiercely.*] Take him away, ma'am, as soon as possible—he's not made of the right material for political life. Oh, what an escape the Party's had! [*He goes out.*

MRS. HOOLEY.

Tim, dear! [*She steals out after* McSHANE.

LADY RIPSTOW.

Mr. Trimble—Mr. Trimble——

TRIMBLE.

Oh!

LADY RIPSTOW.

Pray take me downstairs; Lurgashall has evidently——

DENHAM.

I am here, mother. One moment. Mr. Bompas——

MRS. BOMPAS.

Percy!

BOMPAS.

Well?

DENHAM.

You are going to leave London, to live abroad, I hear.

BOMPAS.

Yes!

DENHAM.

There is one duty which I hope you will perform, sir, before you start.

BOMPAS.

Duty?

DENHAM.

A father's duty—to give Beryl to me, at our marriage.

MRS. BOMPAS.

Berry!

LADY RIPSTOW.

No, no! I forbid it!

BOMPAS.

Lurgashall! After all! After all! [*He sways;* DENHAM *supports him.*] Oh! Lurgashall!

THE END.

Printed by BALLANTYNE HANSON & CO.
London and Edinburgh

A Selection

FROM

MR. WM. HEINEMANN'S LIST.

October, 1891.

Heinemann's 3s. 6d. Novels.

A MARKED MAN. Some Episodes in his Life.
By ADA CAMBRIDGE.
Pall Mall.—"Contains one of the best written stories of a *mésalliance* that is to be found in modern fiction."

IN THE VALLEY. By HAROLD FREDERIC.
Illustrated.
Athenæum.—"A novel deserving to be read."

THE THREE MISS KINGS. By ADA
CAMBRIDGE.
British Weekly.—"A novel to be bought and kept for re-reading on languid summer afternoons or stormy winter evenings."

PRETTY MISS SMITH. By FLORENCE
WARDEN.
Punch.—"Since the 'House on the Marsh,' I have not read a more exciting tale."

A ROMANCE OF THE CAPE FRONTIER.
By BERTRAM MITFORD.
Observer.—"A rattling tale—genial, healthy, and spirited."

THE BONDMAN. By HALL CAINE.
Academy.—"A splendid novel."

A VERY STRANGE FAMILY. By F. W.
ROBINSON.
Glasgow Herald.—"Delightful reading from start to finish."

A MODERN MARRIAGE. By the MARQUISE
CLARA LANZA.
Queen.—"A powerful story."

LOS CERRITOS. A Romance of the Modern
Time. By GERTRUDE FRANKLIN ATHERTON.
Athenæum.—"A decidedly charming romance."

Ibeinemann's International Library.

Edited by EDMUND GOSSE. Price 3*s.* 6*d.* cloth, 2*s.* 6*d.* paper.

New Review.—"If you have any pernicious remnants of literary chauvinism, I hope it will not survive the series of foreign classics of which Mr. William Heinemann, aided by Mr. Edmund Gosse, is publishing translations to the great contentment of all lovers of literature."

Times.—"A venture which deserves encouragement."

** Each Volume has an Introduction specially written by the Editor.

IN GOD'S WAY. From the Norwegian of BJÖRNSTJERNE BJÖRNSON.

Athenæum.—"Without doubt the most important and the most interesting work published during the twelve months. . . . There are descriptions which certainly belong to the best and cleverest things our literature has ever produced."

PIERRE AND JEAN. From the French of GUY DE MAUPASSANT.

Pall Mall Gazette.—"So fine and faultless, so perfectly balanced, so steadily progressive, so clear and simple and satisfying. It is admirable from beginning to end."

THE CHIEF JUSTICE. From the German of KARL EMIL FRANZOS, Author of "For the Right," &c.

New Review.—"Few novels of recent times have a more sustained and vivid human interest."

WORK WHILE YE HAVE THE LIGHT. From the Russian of COUNT TOLSTOY.

Scotsman.—"It is impossible to convey any adequate idea of the simplicity and force with which the work is unfolded."

FANTASY. From the Italian of MATILDE SERAO.

Scottish Leader.—"It is a work of elfish art, a mosaic of life and love, of right and wrong, o: human weakness and strength, and purity and wantonness pieced together in deft and witching precision."

FROTH. From the Spanish of DON ARMANDO PALACIO VALDÉS.

Daily Telegraph.—"Vigorous and powerful in the highest degree. It abounds in forcible delineation of character, and describes scenes with rare and graphic strength."

FOOTSTEPS OF FATE. From the Dutch of
Louis Couperus.
Daily Chronicle.—"A powerfully realistic story, which has
been excellently translated."

PEPITA XIMENEZ. From the Spanish of
Juan Valera.

THE COMMODORE'S DAUGHTERS. From
the Norwegian of Jonas Lie

The Drama.

THE DRAMATIC WORKS OF ARTHUR
W. PINERO. Published in Monthly Parts, each containing a Complete Play, with its Stage History. Price 1s. 6d.
paper cover, 2s. 6d. cloth extra.

PART I. Containing "The Times," a New and Original
Comedy, to be produced at Terry's Theatre, October
1891.

PART II. Containing "The Profligate." With a Portrait.

PART III. Containing "The Cabinet Minister."

₊ To be followed by the Author's other Plays.

NERO AND ACTEA. A Tragedy. By Eric
Mackay, Author of "A Lover's Litanies," and "Love
Letters of a Violinist." Crown 8vo, 5s.

HEDDA GABLER. A Drama in Four Acts.
By Henrik Ibsen. Translated from the Norwegian by
Edmund Gosse. Library edition, with Portrait, small 4to,
5s. Vaudeville Edition, paper, 1s.

₊ Also a limited large paper edition, with three portraits,
21s. net.

THE FRUITS OF ENLIGHTENMENT.
A Comedy in Four Acts. By Lyof Tolstoy. Translated
from the Russian by E. J. Dillon. With an Introduction
by A. W. Pinero, and a Portrait of the Author. Small
4to, 5s

THE PRINCESSE MALEINE. By Maurice
Maeterlinck. Translated by Gerard Harry. With an
Introduction by Oscar Wilde. Small 4to, with a Portrait.
[In the Press

STRAY THOUGHTS. By Ellen Terry.
One Volume, Illustrated. *[In the Press.*

THE LIFE OF HENRIK IBSEN. By
HENRIK JÆGER. Translated by CLARA BELL. With the Verse done into English from the Norwegian original by EDMUND GOSSE. In One Volume, crown 8vo, 6s.

New Works of Fiction.

Ready.

THE SCAPEGOAT. By HALL CAINE, Author
of "The Bondman." In Two Volumes.

MEA CULPA. A Woman's Last Word. By
HENRY HARLAND (Sidney Luska), Author of " As it was Written." In Three Volumes, crown 8vo.

COME FORTH! A Story of the Time of Christ.
By ELIZABETH STUART PHELPS and HERBERT D. WARD. In One Volume, imperial 16mo, 7s. 6d.

THE MASTER OF THE MAGICIANS. A
Novel. By ELIZABETH STUART PHELPS and HERBERT D. WARD. In One Volume, imperial 16mo, 7s. 6d.

THE MOMENT AFTER. A Tale of the
Unseen. By ROBERT BUCHANAN. Popular Edition, crown 8vo, 1s.

Shortly.

THE PENANCE OF PORTIA JAMES.
By TASMA, Author of "Uncle Piper," &c. In One Volume.

MAYONNAISE. By MAARTEN MAARTENS,
Author of "The Sin of Joost Aveling," &c.

WOMAN AND THE MAN. By ROBERT
BUCHANAN. In Two Vols.

INCONSEQUENT LIVES. By J. H. PEARCE, Author of " Esther Pentreath," &c.

DAUGHTERS OF MEN. By HANNAH LYNCH, Author of " The Prince of the Glades," &c.

ACCORDING TO ST. JOHN. By AMÉLIE RIVES. In One Volume.

THE TOWER OF TADDEO. By OUIDA, Author of "Two Little Wooden Shoes," &c.

MAMMON. By Mrs. ALEXANDER, Author of "The Wooing O't," &c. In Three Vols.

LITTLE JOHANNES. A Fairy Tale. By F. VAN EEDEN. Translated from the Dutch, by CLARA BELL, with an Introduction by ANDREW LANG, and Illustrations by DUDLEY HARDY. In One Volume.

ORIOLE'S DAUGHTER. By JESSIE FOTHER-GILL, Author of "The First Violin," &c. In Three Vols.

COME LIVE WITH ME AND BE MY LOVE. By ROBERT BUCHANAN.

THE WHITE FEATHER. By TASMA. In Three Vols.

NOT ALL IN VAIN. By ADA CAMBRIDGE, Author of " A Marked Man," &c.

A BATTLE AND A BOY. By BLANCHE WILLIS HOWARD, Author of " Guenn," &c.

Miscellaneous.

THE LITTLE MANX NATION. By HALL CAINE, Author of " The Bondman." Crown 8vo, cloth, 3s. 6d.; paper, 2s. 6d.

GIRLS AND WOMEN. By E. Chester,

Pott 8vo, 2s. 6d., or gilt extra, 3s. 6d.
Contents : An Aim in Life. Health. A Practical Education.
Self-support—Shall Girls Support Themselves? Self-support—
How shall Girls Support Themselves? Occupation for the Rich.
Culture. The Essentials of a Lady. The Problem of Charity.
The Essentials of a Home. Hospitality. Bric-à-Brac. Emo-
tional Women. A Question of Society. Narrow Lives. Con-
clusion.

GOSSIP IN A LIBRARY. By Edmund Gosse.

16mo.   *[In the Press.*
Contents: The Library. Camden's Britannia. The Mirror
for Magistrates. A Poet in Prison. Death's Duel. Gerard's
Herbal. Pharamond. A Volume of Old Plays. A Censor of
Poets. Amasia. Love and Business. What Ann Lang read.
Cats. The Song to David. Pompey the Little. John Buncle.
Beau Nash. The Natural History of Selborne. The Diary of
a Lover of Literature. Peter Bell and his Tormentors. The
Fancy. Ultracrepidarius. The Duke of Rutland's Poems.
The Scarlet Letter. Ionica. The Shaving of Shagpat.

WOMAN—THROUGH A MAN'S EYE-

GLASS. By Malcolm C. Salaman. With Illustrations by Dudley Hardy. Fcap. 8vo, 3s. 6d.
                                                [In the Press.

THE COMING TERROR, and other Essays

and Letters. By Robert Buchanan. Second Edition.
Demy 8vo, 12s. 6d.

THE WORKS OF HEINRICH HEINE.

Translated by Charles G. Leland, F.R.L.S., M.A.
Volume I.—Florentine Nights, Schnabelewopski. The
Rabbi of Bacharach, and Shakespeare's Maidens and
Women. Volumes II. and III., Pictures of Travel. In
Two Volumes. Volume IV., The Book of Songs. Volumes
V. and VI., Germany. In Two Volumes. Crown 8vo, 5s.
each.

DE QUINCEY MEMORIALS. Edited by
ALEXANDER H. JAPP, LL.D., F.R.S.E. In Two Volumes, demy 8vo, with portrait, 30s. net.

THE POSTHUMOUS WORKS OF
THOMAS DE QUINCEY Edited by ALEXANDER H. JAPP, LL.D., F.R.S.E. Volume I. Suspiria de Profundis, and other Essays. Crown 8vo, 6s.

THE GENTLE ART OF MAKING ENE-
MIES. By J. M'NEILL WHISTLER. In One Volume, pott 4to, 10s. 6d. Also, 150 Copies on Hand-made Paper, Numbered and Signed by the Author, £2 2s. each.

IMPERIAL GERMANY. A Critical Study of
Fact and Character. By SIDNEY WHITMAN. Crown 8vo, cloth, 2s. 6d.; paper 2s.

DENMARK : Its History, Topography, Language,
Literature, Fine Arts, Social Life, and Finance. Edited by H. WEITMEYER. With Coloured Map. In One Volume, 8vo, 12s. 6d. Dedicated by permission to H.R.H. the Princess of Wales.

THE GENESIS OF THE UNITED
STATES. A Narrative of the Movement in England 1605–1616, which resulted in the Plantation of North America by Englishmen. By ALEXANDER BROWN, F.R.H.S., &c. &c. In Two Volumes, 8vo, with numerous maps, plans, portraits, autographs, &c., £3 13s. 6d.

THE GARDEN'S STORY; or, Pleasures and
Trials of an Amateur Gardener. By G. H. ELLWANGER. With an Introduction by the Rev. C. WOLLEY DOD. In One Volume, fcap. 8vo, illustrated, 5s.

THE PASSION PLAY AT OBERAM-
MERGAU, 1890. By F. W. FARRAR, D.D., F.R.S., Archdeacon and Canon of Westminster. In One Volume, 4to, cloth, 2s. 6d.

THE LABOUR MOVEMENT IN

AMERICA. By RICHARD T. ELY, Ph.D., Associate in
Political Economy, Johns Hopkins University. In One
Volume, crown 8vo, 5*s*.

ARABIC AUTHORS: A Manual of Arabian

History and Literature. By F. F. ARBUTHNOT, M.R.A.S.,
Author of "Early Ideas," and "Persian Portraits." In
One Volume, post 8vo, 10*s*.

IDLE MUSINGS : Essays in Social Mosaic. By

E. CONDER GRAY, Author of "Wise Words and Loving
Deeds," &c. &c. In One Volume, crown 8vo, 6*s*.

Heinemann's Scientific Handbooks.

GEODESY. By J. HOWARD GORE. Small

crown 8vo, illustrated, cloth, 5*s*.

MANUAL OF ASSAYING GOLD, SILVER,

COPPER, and LEAD ORES. By WALTER LEE BROWN,
B.Sc. With a Chapter on the ASSAYING OF FUEL, by
A. B. GRIFFITHS, Ph.D., F.R.S., F.C.S. Small crown
8vo, illustrated, cloth, 7*s*. 6*d*.
Colliery Guardian.—"A delightful and fascinating book."

THE PHYSICAL PROPERTIES OF

GASES. By ARTHUR L. KIMBALL. Small crown 8vo,
illustrated, cloth, 5*s*.
Chemical News.—"The man of culture who wishes for a
general and accurate acquaintance with the physical properties
of gases will find in Mr. Kimball's work just what he requires."

HEAT AS A FORM OF ENERGY. By

Professor R. H. THURSTON. Small crown 8vo, illustrated,
cloth, 5*s*.
Chemical News.—This work will prove both welcome and
useful."